T0106221

Take Me From the Darkside

Take Me From the Darkside

Janice Melton Ruggiero

Copyright © 2011 by Janice Melton Ruggiero.

ISBN: Softcover   978-1-4535-0973-9
               Ebook   978-1-4535-0974-6

All rights reserved. No part of this book may be reproduced or transmitted in any form or by any means, electronic or mechanical, including photocopying, recording, or by any information storage and retrieval system, without permission in writing from the copyright owner.

This book was printed in the United States of America.

To order additional copies of this book, contact:
Xlibris Corporation
1-888-795-4274
www.Xlibris.com
Orders@Xlibris.com
57793

DEDICATED TO THOSE WHO STRUGGLE WITH DRUG AND ALCOHOL ADDICTIONS

I simply want to comfort, if only one suffering through withdrawal, in a comforting-easy-to-read-empathetic fashion. A book such as this *might have made a difference* for me to struggle through the full 28 days of recovery during my most recent rehab stay, and instead of leaving the facility remaining an addict, I *may have left sober.*

Names and places are fictionalized in this book for reasons personal to the author. But this book is a non-fictional testimonial account of my recovery from vicodin (opioids) and my recovery from prior addictions and alcoholism that I suffered with in my life by discovering, acknowledging, and resolving the core reasons and triggers that led me into the abyss of drug abuse and alcohol abuse.

The purpose and goal of this book is to bring hope to those presently suffering with vicodin abuse or forms of abuse of any narcotics. In my past I was addicted to alcohol, so I pray this book also brings hope for recovery to those presently suffering with any form of alcoholism.

My immediate family, special friends, churches, and the medical doctor that saved my life is not written in fictionalized names, but their real identities are given by permission from them. I want to lead people especially who are suffering from painkiller pill abuse to the doctor that helped me, and the only way I can do that is by giving her true identity. So I pray that those who need help now to rid their lives of opioids or opiates will call her to begin their medical recovery process.

A personal thank you to:

Dr. Dora Dixie of Near South Health Center.

I refer Dr. Dora Dixie of the Near South Health Center for those who seriously are ready to stop using opiates or opioids and want to live a sober life. The following is the address and phone number for outpatient treatment by Dr. Dixie:

Near South Health Center
3525 South Michigan Avenue
Chicago, Illinois 60653
312 945 4010

Dr. Dixie offers a recovery program medically monitored on an out-patient basis or at-home detox, prescribing Suboxone treatment. This medication contains buprenorphine hydrochloride, which works to reduce the symptoms of opiate or opioid dependence. It also contains one other ingredient called Naloxone to guard against misuse.

Suboxone is less tightly controlled than methadone because it has a lower potential for abuse and is less dangerous in an overdose. As patients progress on therapy, your doctor may write a prescription for a take-home supply of the medication. (*Embrace Treatment Regain Control, Suboxone, provided as an educational service by Reckitt Benckiser Pharmaceuticals, Inc.*).

Finally this would be the medication treatment after five years of failing that helped kick the vicodin addiction permanently for me! I can honestly testify that Dr. Dora Dixie saved my life!

I would definitely recommend treating those suffering any opiate or opioid addiction to call Dr. Dora Dixie.

This doctor worked best for me after unsuccessfully attempting to complete two (2) 28 day in-stay rehabilitation programs, one in Florida and later, in Illinois. Both of these rehabilitation centers overdosed me on various psychotropic medications such as symbiax, zyprexa and prozac. Dr. Dora Dixie knew the proper medication that would work to stop my addiction while not ignoring my other mental disorders.

In my case, the Suboxone simultaneously helped me to go cold turkey on vicodin and adderall!

Dr. Dixie will refer you to psychiatric or psychological help to supplement your recovery process as you take the Suboxone. She highly recommends attending A.A. and N.A. Recovery meetings and will talk with you as you meet with her about your recovery actions. She is the type of doctor that truly cares that you are seeking as much help as possible to prevent falling back into using any forms of alcohol or drugs.

Before you can even concentrate on meetings and improving your regular life duties involving family and work, you have to physically become well. This is the purpose of my placing the referral of Dr. Dora Dixie in the very beginning of my book.

Sometimes you will receive this medication at rehab centers but not under the personal care that Dr. Dixie delicately administers. For example, when I was given the Suboxone at the latest rehab facility I attended, where I was not even explained about what I was given, I was taken off of the medicine much too quickly; and therefore my relapse was already taking place in my mind before I even left the detox unit. If you take the medicine under Dr. Dixie properly while attending your meetings, and seeking a sponsor to be accountable to, and of course, if you are serious about your sobriety, you will succeed. If I could do it after many years of failing my sobriety, you can too!

My recipe for sobriety from opioid addiction:

- First seeing an addiction recovery medical doctor who is certified in administering opiate/opioid addiction withdrawal recovery medication such as Suboxone;
- seeing an addiction recovery psychiatrist (fictionally re-named Griffin in this book) *continually to discover, acknowledge and resolve the core reasons for your ever using drugs or alcohol;*
- attending daily-weekly A.A. or N.A. meetings, and seeking an A.A. or N.A. sponsor to be accountable to such as upholding a regimented meeting agenda;
- attending a weekly worship service, and at least one church fellowship group meeting with people who are non-alcohol and non-drug users;
- establishing and maintaining a true friendship with at least one dependable Christian sober friend;
- establishing and maintaining a healthy diet including a lot of water and exercise to attain natural energy

Introduction

Nothing will work for you, until you are truly sick and tired of being sick and tired. That is not a cliché to take lightly. I at first did not think much of it when I heard others testify to this state of mind and physical condition during A.A. and N.A. speaker meetings.

It is not until you are truly ready to be sober and submissive to God, that you will become sober. You cannot fool yourself. You must go to meetings with the sincere attitude that you want to finally live the sober life. You must be willing, and if you are willing, you will be able.

It is a shame that some of us have to go through so much guilt, shame, and physical decline before we come to terms that we have to give up the carnal substances that we relied on to take us through life.

But it is when we have a spiritual awakening, the guilt and shame will finally diminish. We come to believe that God forgives us and accepts us just as we are, and our sins are forgiven. This will happen for you, as it has for me, if you are ready to stop for good. Once you feel the joy of sobriety, and you have developed a solid network of good sober friends, you will no longer allow the dark side to drag you back; but you press forward to the bright side—the way in which God created you to enjoy His gift of life.

If one overcomes a drug or alcohol addiction, and can contribute to the world's defense against the number one most vicious and greedy killer of our world's youth by sharing her or his testimony, then I believe that person's efforts to reach others should be attempted. Since I have been encouraged by the testimonies of others, I wanted to give back in the same manner.

I know what anyone who is withdrawing from opioids, (e.g., hydrocodone or oxycodone), or opiates, (e.g., morphine and codeine), is going through.

During my first in-stay rehab in Florida, when I was desperately deprived of being able to attain sleep, God gave me nightly sleep after I prayed to Him to work a miracle in my life. That same night, after faithfully praying to God as I know Him, I fell asleep around 10:30 p.m., as if the Holy Spirit placed a blanket to rest over my body; and I awoke at 5:45 a.m. to the beautiful sound of chirping birds. From that night through to the end of my graduating the rehab program, I slept and awoke *at the same time* each day—just like that! For me, it was nothing short of a miracle from God to help me make it through the treacherous anxiety that haunts those who are going through withdrawal.

If you are in withdrawal in a rehab or in your own home, faithfully pray for God's intervention to help you to rid your mind of the aftermath that comes upon us from stopping our addictions, and He will. He knows you are bettering your life, and He knows the pain that you are enduring to become a better person. So, He will help, if you pray *in faith that He is listening to you.*

I profess the A.A. and N.A. (Alcoholics Anonymous and Narcotics Anonymous) Steps of Recovery because they make sense to me, and they did carry me through *understanding why*

I was using. Although I'd never describe any specific testimonies of others due to the anonymity principles that A.A./N.A. are founded upon, I do write in a generalized, respectful manner, what I learned from attending meetings.

In this book, I reference the *Life Recovery Bible*, which integrates the Twelve Steps of A.A. and N.A. throughout a modern language version of the *King James Bible*, for the purpose of reinforcing the Steps in light of God's Word. The Steps are repeated numerously throughout the *Life Recovery Bible* as they relate to specific Bible passages.

Even if one (1) out of 20 can be influenced by my testimony, as the testimonial stories in A.A. and N.A. books have helped me, thus I felt a purpose in sharing. It is not the drug or alcoholic counselors and psychologists . . . it is our peers, other addicts and alcoholics, whom we desire to hear from or read from, while we are recovering. A more in—depth recovery story about opioid addiction recovery is what I needed to read while in two different rehabs, but I could not find this type of book that I am now writing to those who may have similar addiction recovery struggles.

There are not enough published testimonial writings of overcoming the evil, intrusive destruction of drug addiction, in the origin and structure composed in this book. I desired this kind of reading after going through detoxification, but was at least fortunate enough to attain a copy of an A.A. book. At both rehab centers it was encouraging for me to begin perceiving A.A. and N.A. meetings much more respectively and seriously.

It is my prayer that my recovery process as told in this book may influence other recovering addicts or alcoholics to share their stories with alcohol and drug rehab facility libraries, in order to offer more of a variety of reading to delicately aid patients in successful rehab stays and exits.

I strongly feel that a more empathetic reading selection could have encouraged me to remain sober after my first in-stay rehab experience, thus omitting the need for me to go through another in-stay rehab experience a few years later. This type of book was the "something" that was missing, at least for me, to get through those awful painful nights.

I remember giving my only Bible, which I thankfully brought with me, to a co-patient while in the detoxification unit of my second rehab facility stay in Illinois. I later gave out other religious oriented self-help books on quitting drugs and alcohol to fellow patients, who, like me, were also disappointed that the facility had little if nothing comforting to offer its patients to read at night.

I was determined to bring more reading materials with me to the second rehab facility, since I earlier learned while in the first facility in Florida, that the library was insufficient in recovery—type readings for its patients.

Co-patients in the second rehab facility in Illinois found the reading materials I brought, such as sobriety-gratification books based on God's Scriptures, to be so helpful, that I could not get them back. Patients were passing the books around, and some told me that the supplemental readings helped them to get through their hardest days and nights.

I wished that I had brought more books when I was at the first rehab facility in Florida. But since I had no books to supplement my co-patients' struggles, I would write encouraging poems for each specific patient enlightening them of their personal talents and gifts after getting to know them during group discussions. I wanted to use my gift of writing to encourage those who shared the same fear and guilt as myself.

It takes a keenly sensitive book that a suffering reader is capable of relating to; and furthermore, receiving comfort from, while going through the aches, the sweating, and anxiety of withdrawal. This book presents itself in an easy to read and interesting fashion, taking in concern the reader—the addict. It will be exhilarating encouragement and hope for you when you have made up your mind that enough is enough.

I am sure my story is similar to many of you out there that just cannot quit taking whichever form of opioids is your choice. Although since my story relates to prior addictions to other drugs and alcohol, I am hopeful it will include an encouragement to all addicts and alcoholics truly wanting to secure a successful recovery to a new way of life.

It is very difficult to concentrate when one is suffering through withdrawal. In my case, it was vicodin abuse that first brought me into my first rehab facility But as earlier mentioned, I needed to be sure to not fall back on former abuses that had intruded upon my life on and off for more than 20 years.

Whether you are withdrawing from any painkillers such as vicodin, oxycotin, oxycodone, or heroine, I do understand how you are feeling—so perhaps you may be able to read my book and get some tips of help that will save you as I was saved.

Vicodin painkillers were the most fearful life-destructive drug I had ever allowed myself to get addicted to, and if I beat it, you can too!

My goal is that this is the type of book that the suffering reader can comprehend from beginning to end, and second, can visualize his and her very own rainbow on the top of their journey in making the 12 Steps of Recovery.

During the long days while I was in rehab facilities, I wished I would have been given time-out to curl up and attain empathy for my suffering, from a comforting writer who understood *exactly* what I was going through: how I was sweating, how I was scared to eat because I could not hold anything down, how I was scared to go to sleep, and how I was scared to awake . . . if I ever could sleep. This was my drive to write this testimonial account of my story. I hope it will be accepted by rehab facilities for helping in reinforcing the addict or alcoholic to make it through each day as they progress through the Program.

There were other mental disorder medications that were erroneously administered to me by the nurses of both rehab centers, but not to their fault. Anti-psychotic medications were ill-diagnosed by the psychiatrists that resulted in my mental health decline, and resulted in my vicodin addiction becoming more explosive after I was released from both facilities.

Therefore, my second purpose in writing this book is that the rehab facilities equip their staff with a better ratio than one psychiatrist to 100 or 200 patients which was the poor dilemma in both facilities where I stayed.

If my mental health conditions and migraine headache conditions were simultaneously treated during my detox, I believe I could have done the next phase of group discussion work more successfully. The first rehab center did take into consideration my ADD and ADHD disorders, as well as my migraine ailments, and therefore I made it through the 28-day Program.

But I still was misdiagnosed with various anti-psychotic medicines that affected my retaining sobriety after being released. I was overdosed with symbiax and zyprexa that affected my state of mind, even though I made it through the 28-day program. I believe these misdiagnosed anti-psychotics affected my mental chemistry to affect my sobriety—I remember becoming more anxious than I had ever been prior to entering the first rehab facility.

A few years later, upon entering my second rehab facility, my mental disorders and migraines were completely disregarded during detox, and affected my performance in the following workgroup sessions that follow as part of the Program.

So this rehab outcome was even worse than the first time around in Florida. At least the first rehab did not ignore my prior mental disorders, and even tried to help with my anxiety levels, although they misdiagnosed the medications. This happens. So I must say, I was more grateful to the first rehab's level of empathy for its patients versus my second time around at the second facility in Illinois.

Without proper psychiatric care due to a shockingly poor psychiatrist-to-patient ratio, my outlook for recovery success was dim, and I could not concentrate and participate progressively within group settings.

How was I to continue progressive treatment from my addictions while suffering from other unassociated or associated illnesses to my addictions? At the second rehab facility, I was harshly and repeatedly scolded that I needed to be "cold turkey" on all drugs. Without migraine medication, for example, my blood pressure dropped as the migraine pain increased to the point of my needing to be admitted into emergency hospital care outside of the rehab facility.

The first rehab center did have better psychiatrist empathy for the patients, but the second rehab facility's psychiatrist only knew his patients through reading charts. You learn as you go through rehab center trials, and it is in my right to criticize an extreme failure in vital psychiatric staff at both rehab facilities.

Since these facilities may have improved their psychiatric staff since my stays, I felt it best not to name the facilities.

Anyhow, I must seriously argue with some rehab centers' rules and guidelines about taking patients off *all* medications while undergoing treatment for their addictions. I realize the rehab administrative staff has researched statistics for coming to their decisions on how they will medicate or non-medicate addicts; but I painfully argue that ALL mental and physical conditions of addicts should be given more careful analysis, *and if necessary be medically treated, e.g., for migraine headaches, as long as the addict is respectively remaining submissive to abstain from the abusive substances.*

I felt that neither rehab place was affective for my recovery, due in large part that only one (1) psychiatrist was on site for *more than 100 patients*, thus allowing very limited time for one-on-one psychiatrist-patient sessions. More one-on-one psychiatric treatments were detrimentally needed for many suffering addicts. This truthfully was the situation at both rehabs where I attended. And if psychiatric help was poorly staffed in an Illinois and in a Florida facility, you cannot help but think this must be the situation at many more facilities across the nation. I hope today that patients are given more psychiatric care.

Many of my inpatient peers complained how they felt mistreated to be given only a half-hour of time to talk to the psychiatrist, once per week. This was in the first rehab place I stayed—the somewhat kinder staffed center.

But the second rehab place was ridiculously administered simply in the length of time a patient had to wait to see a psychiatrist on a one-on-one basis. And it would be a waste of time. Psychiatrists relied on patients' charts almost exclusively.

Additionally, this second trial facility I speak of, gave no consideration to suffering ailments unrelated to the patients' addictions. Then with very little knowledge of the patient, the psychiatrist would prescribe an anti-psychotic, that in my case was prozac, which intruded dangerously on my struggle for sobriety.

I was messed up worse than ever after this second rehab trial, and after being rushed into an emergency hospital outside of the facility during my rehab stay, I am now grateful that I left. I believe I may have died had I stayed on longer than the 10 days that was the most difficult suffering of my life to go through.

There were sufficient one-on-one therapist sessions at both facilities, as well as group sessions with therapists available; but this was insufficient for the special patients who had physical and mental ailments that needed proper medications prescribed *to supplement their addiction recoveries.*

I remember walking in the one and only available psychiatrist office on site in the Florida facility, and meeting him for the first time. He said he could only give me ten minutes of his time because he had 200 other patients to see. I hoped that he was exaggerating, but to my discovery later, he was not far off from the facts.

Perhaps he thought because I was in there as an addict, I was just naturally stupid, and not intelligent enough to realize that he was incriminating himself and his place of work. I was shocked and confused. I told him that I was told during my pre-admittance interview call with an administrative staff member, that I would be able to see a personal psychiatrist as often as necessary. He simply apologized, and said he had to make a vacation trip, so he really needed to hurry through a huge list of patients.

I would advise those entering rehabs to not count on what you are promised will be done for you in the pre-admittance interview calls. They may say you can take certain medications, for example for migraines, and then once you are there, you are stripped of the medications that you thought you could take.

During both pre-admittance interview calls before going to two rehab centers, I was assured psychiatric help and medication help that became a trauma to attain once I was admitted. These type of stresses make your recovery all the more difficult. These stresses, in my own opinion, contributed to my rehab stays turning out to be unsuccessful.

I felt angry that more psychiatrists were not hired on staff to help prescribe and carefully monitor patients with prior mental disorders and prior physical ailments. Ignored mental and physical disorders aside from a patient's addiction made a negative impact on me as well as other co—patients' successfully completing the 12 Step Recovery Program. I am a living testimony to this—yes, my addictions were treated, but not other contributing mental and physical factors affecting my addictions. Therefore, in my case, both inpatient rehab stays failed.

Although, I am grateful to both rehab stays for the *trial and error prescriptions of anti-psychotic medications to rule out those medications that were hurtful to me,* so that they would never again be diagnosed for me in the future.

In my own research, these type of psychotropic medications *are a trial and error process that is unique to each individual; and it truly is not fair to fully blame the psychiatrist for trying to get the exact chemistry match per patient per medication to successfully help that patient, especially if the patient has an addictive personality.* So I do want to contribute some defense and not all blame for what happened in my case, and probably in the case of other rehab patients. There were therapists and nurses that were absolutely wonderful at the rehabs that I must not exclude from thanking in this book.

I am not against rehab facilities, but I am against any misleading information that is permitted to be discussed with patients during the pre-admittance interview calls. I would hope that facilities would be honest in explaining their rules, so the patient may choose the proper facility that works best for his or her addiction as well as his or her mental and physical ailments, aside from their addictions.

I gained wonderful friendships at the rehab facilities and spiritual encouragement from caring people that I am grateful I had the opportunity to experience. So I do want to thank the rehab facilities across the country. I just felt a need to write general honest criticism where it needed to be pointed out for successful outcomes to those patients entering rehabs no matter where they may be.

The addictive patient makes it very difficult to get the right psychotropic or anti-depressant medication that will work uniquely for him or her.

Two of my co-patients did die upon being released from one of the facilities I attended. Yes, two patients died shortly after being released from the same facility during the same 28 day program I attended.

But it is not necessary to go into that account, but I mention it in order to demonstrate the poor psychiatric attention available in some of the most expensive and highly referred rehabs.

Hopefully their psychiatric care has improved, as well as their library inventories, by the time this book is published.

TAKE ME FROM THE DARKSIDE . . .

Glorifies God for His ingenious ways of using sober addicts and alcoholics to exemplify to others the joyful living that commences from sober living;

Exposes Satan's worldly prey upon our youth to deceive them into thinking that partying on drugs and alcohol is a social experience that they just cannot bear to miss out in life, less they regret it later;

Uplifts a true appreciation for the loved ones of addicts and alcoholics—an encouragement to the addict and alcoholic to take help from their loved ones now while they are alive and willing to give their support;

Celebrates the unprecedented lifelong joy to commence for the addict and alcoholic and those in the addict's or alcoholic's inner circle, once the peaks of their recovery climb are beneath their feet;

Gives thanks to the genuinely faithful and dedicated counselors, therapists, psychologists, psychiatrists and administrators in Recovery Programs;

Honors the gracious volunteer outreach and the consistent, disciplined chairing of meetings by devoted A.A. and N.A. sponsors and members everywhere;

Expresses love to A.A. and N.A. members who tell the new comers: "Keep coming back!" These devoted members, who fill the meeting rooms, are as vital to the A.A. and N.A. first-comers as water to the sustainment of humanity . . .

a premise for a sober life . . . my father

. . . his consistent way of life that I had my entire life to look up to . . . since I was a little girl . . . set examples for me . . . I just never realized it . . . never acted on it. Personal inspiration I was fortunate to have from one who never took a pill or a drink to approach life's difficulties, and who naturally outwitted any opposing forces that attempted to obstruct his path.

He already had six family members to take care of as a young boy, and yet still made us, his own children with my mother, to raise with no fear. He did what was right by God: to marry my mother to procreate—which is the Bible reasoning for God creating the covenant of marriage.

And yet I was a problem child, and he still stuck by my side with no fear. I owe my life to my father and mother for encouraging me that I was always better than what I thought of myself. God worked through my father, mother, sister and caring friends to get me through the addictions.

At first when you are a teenager you think that partying is the coolest thing and attractive to gain popularity. But actually, to the smart boys and girls with class and intelligence, I learned the hard way that when they look upon the drunk or drugged teenagers, they are totally and completely turned off by their stupidity.

Wise children, teenagers, and adults do not find getting high or drunk attractive. If you want to find the right partner in life, do not fool yourself into thinking you look cooler by getting high or drunk. I learned the hard way, as many of my youthful friends did.

Satan will always find ways to deceive, even some of the normally wiser of the crowd, to think that the partying road is the way to not miss out on the fun times while you're young, but there are too many beautiful ways to spend our short lives on Earth that do not hurt us or make us feel guilty about ourselves—and those ways are choosing to enjoy your life by going God's way. This way, you are rewarded with good days and good nights, not sick days and sick nights. You save money, and you make a future for yourself that will make your parents proud.

A woman and man look for dependable partners in life, and this makes for successful marriages and families. I am glad I now am on the right side and not blind—sided by Satan's deceit any longer.

Even if you are middle-aged, once you are sober, you will be surprised the youth that God will restore in your body, mind, and soul. God is good to those who choose His path.

Once you know that you are a helpless addict, you naturally feel worthless—it is a vicious downslide of self remorse. But my loved ones never let me slip to the bottom of the ditch. And God used my father as the cornerstone of our family structure. Not only for his immediate family—my mom, me and my sister; but for his family before I came into the world. He kept us all on the right path—his immediate and his extended family.

Yes, I truly believe my father and mother make the proper couple in marriage sanctified by God. Sanctification is not a word to use lightly. So to say that God has sanctified (anointed through the blood of Christ's death) my parents, comes from the deepest depths of my heart, and the most sincere and gracious comment I can make upon them as parents and as leaders of a family structure. They are caregivers (and yes, there is such a term).

So I want to thank my parents and sister (who I term as my guardian angel, because God sends angels in various forms for those whom He chooses to protect) for not allowing me to hit rock bottom from my addictions.

Hey, it's in my blood to become as strong as my parents. I just never thought about it . . . but then drugs demise one's wisdom. I finally begun to draw on my physical and mental gene reserves once my mind was clear . . . and I began feeling naturally good . . . like my father had always tried to tell me it could be.

My sister consistently encouraged me, even more tenaciously after my husband abandoned me. This was the time that I could have fallen into the worse addictive abyss ever; and yet, miraculously, I became stronger than ever—quitting the two hardest drugs at the same time—that is, vicodin and adderall. Those who have been addicted to these drugs know what I am talking about. They are extremely difficult to stop.

I now live with ADD and ADHD without any specific medication for these disorders, and I am living sober through fellowship in God's church, and through the 12 Steps of Recovery. And you can too.

I am so proud that I have family leaders who unlike me never allowed drugs to enter their lives, let alone take over their lives. So, those of you out there who have loved ones that are reaching out to you—do not let go of their hand. You may slip by a few fingers, but never let go of their hand. It took a long time for me to accept their help, because as long as you use, your mind will never be clear. You cannot see what is available to help you because you are still under the influence. The sweating, the aches, the pain in your body when you awake, the hot to cold flashes, the paranoia, can all go away. You can take control of making your body and mind right again; and the first thing to help you withdraw properly from the vicodin is through the medication I mention in this book.

Then God will bring friends to blanket you when you have cold flashes or to place the cool rag upon your head when you have the headaches. Once you have made up your mind to finally quit, God will bring the comfort you need whether in the rehab or in your home. Pray in faith and you shall be answered—and you will gain the best friends you have never realized you could have in life. This is all just the beginning of your revival. After your revival, the joy will commence.

Although, for adderall, I must say I did not take any medication to withdraw; BUT, the same medication that helped me to get off of vicodin, fortunately and surprisingly helped me to get off the adderall. So please read my recipe for sobriety if you want to get out from the dark side of life—this is not the way God wants you to live—and now I know. I am 47 years old, so it is never too late for you to stop what you are using and appreciate yourself and to turn your life around.

I scared my husband most as he witnessed me go through the withdrawals, and he was the initial drive toward my journey to sobriety. I was forced to see myself as a person that was scaring loved ones, while I only worried about where and how I would maintain my opioid supply. You cannot begin to feel the hurt you cause others while you are obsessed in making yourself feel good. While I took my pills, my loved ones took nothing. As horrible as the pain of withdrawal can become, I now believe it is more painful for the addict's loved ones who are unknowledgeable about what they are witnessing become of their loved ones, and feel helpless to do anything for them.

Step One

WE ADMITTED THAT WE WERE POWERLESS OVER OUR PROBLEMS—THAT OUR LIVES HAD BECOME UNMANAGEABLE.

But I don't have the strength to endure. I have nothing to live for. Do I have the strength of a stone? Is my body made of bronze? No, I am utterly helpless, without any chance of success.

(Job 6:11-13) Life Recovery Bible

Like witnessing the sun rise for the first time, I realized that if I am sincere about getting help, and working the Program, then I may actually be able to live entirely sober, like my parents. The Illinois rehab did not make me sober, but it did make me determined to find a solution to my problem. Step 1 was no longer a theory to me, but an action that I must take—a resolve that I must make in order to survive. I acknowledged to myself how desperately I needed a workable program to rescue me from the overkill of my vicodin addiction. I re-committed in accountability to my fellow N.A. and A.A. members in respect and self gratification at which I now approach this first vital step of the Program.

Although I had been taking vicodin, a form of opioid, for more than five years, it really did not hit me until I came out of the

Illinois rehab that my addiction was much more powerful than I had believed in the past.

I made the unpleasant call to my parents to pick me up from the Illinois rehab after having stayed only ten days into the Program. My husband refused to pick me up because he believed I was not trying hard enough to finish the Program. I forgive him because he could not understand what truly made me leave prematurely; because if he had understood, he would not have ignored my repeated phone calls of distress.

I was suffering from migraine headaches that disabled me from attending program group sessions. Although Illinois rehab's program structure was much more regimented than I had imagined, I still desired to finish, but simply could not go through it, due to unrelenting migraine headaches. Daily group sessions (starting with breakfast) mandated line-up attendance from 6 a.m. to 9 p.m. with 15 to 20 minute breaks in between. The director made no exceptions for napping, unless a patient became seriously ill; and if allowed, it would be monitored under a strict time allotment.

I was even watched over as I went to the bathroom, which was quite disturbing as a woman. And during detox, I had a huge window in my door, which is meant only for patients that are suicidal. So, it was very disturbing to know that any man could see me in my distress, including throwing up. This total invasion of privacy made my detox recovery all the more disruptive and unprogressive.

I was allowed two naps at two different intervals, but it would not subdue the pain. Headache medication, such as Excedrin, was prohibited, even if the levels of pain escalated into migraine impairment. I tried to accept their rules and graciously swallowed the permitted aspirin, but unfortunately it would not subdue the physical distraction I suffered from the ongoing migraine pain. I simply could not physically hold my head up to join the others for breakfast, let alone to follow readings in discussion group.

After being admitted into the emergency center of a nearby Illinois hospital, I was immediately administered prescription migraine headache medication. Upon my return to the rehab facility, I met with the executive director to explain in detail to him how his staff assured me during my pre-admittance phone interview that I would be allowed to take Imitrex for migraine headaches while under their care. He apologized saying that his staff simply misinformed me. According to him, they only administer certain aspirin because they do not want the patients taking other headache medications that contain even the slightest amount of amphetamine.

He did not seem to realize that my migraine condition co-treatment was an important factor that I had pre-considered for treatment approval as I carefully decided which rehabilitation center I would attend. Additionally, I informed him of what the emergency doctor said about the rehab's ill-regard to my headache sufferings: "You should be allowed to take Imitrex medication, because if monitored properly it would not interfere with your recovery from vicodin addiction, and would contribute to a successful recovery." Unfortunately the hospital doctor made no impression upon the Illinois rehab executive director, and he recommended it was probably better for me to find a treatment center that would have empathy to my migraine headache critical sufferings, and allow the Imitrex. The alternative would be to call the ambulance and go to the hospital emergency room each and every time I suffered with dehydration and low blood pressure during my Illinois rehab stay, due to the migraines. I found the alternative to be insensitive and sort of ridiculous.

Although I did receive an apology by the Illinois rehab facility administrator that they were sorry they could not alter there strict rules—perhaps I was one of few with this migraine condition . . . I left his office feeling disappointed and confused. I did not want to give up the fight. So, I still tried to hold out as long as I could. I tried to attend as many sessions as possible, until the pain once again became unbearable. I drank more water at the facility to help prevent dehydration, which I learned is a major trigger for migraine attacks. I kept my head down on the table during group sessions, hoping the pain would gradually cease . . . but it did not. I was not strong enough to rise above the intruding migraines.

I initially called my spouse to try to attain his empathy; but he refused to come to check on me, let alone take me out of there to safety. I know that he could not have understood what I was going through. He would not even accept the limited calls I could make on my calling card. I do forgive him, because he could not understand how badly I wanted to stay, and instead, judged me as a quitter. That hurt quite severely, because I thought my husband knew me better.

My husband ended up divorcing me in large part due to my failure at completing the Illinois rehab 28-day Program. He agreed with the Illinois rehab executive director and administrator's strict rules and limitations on medications. An addict does need to withdraw from the addictive behavior triggers as we learn in group sessions, but does that mean the addict cannot have medication to assist in the withdrawal pain? These are matters of medical rehabilitation that I truly believe need to be researched more thoroughly, and thus is in part the purpose of me sharing my testimony by this book.

The rehab center I attended two years prior in Florida was not as strict on helping addicts who needed medications that would provide respite care as they would make progress in therapy sessions. But like Illinois rehab, the psychiatric care at the Florida rehab, was insufficient and the cause for over-dosing patients with anti-psychotic medications.

I made the 28 days at the Florida rehab, and received my coin of recovery, and my marriage improved temporarily. My husband came to stay a few days at the beach with me to celebrate my recovery.

But *the core reasons* for my using vicodin were unprofessionally addressed, and thus, the reason I ended up using vicodin again; and accelerating to excessive adderall use, which prompted my re-committing two years later to the Illinois rehab facility to attempt to attain the proper psychiatric help to *resolve the deep rooted reasons for my addictive nature.*

But I know that I truly did try to hold out as long as I could . . . and it hurt me deeply that my husband perceived the Illinois rehab event as a complete failure. My leaving the Center against my husband's wishes impacted his decision to finalize his year-long pending divorce from me.

As I was riding home in the backseat of my parents' car in August of 2008, from the Illinois rehab, I thought of how they, my parents, have always been my role models, *for living life on life's terms.* That is, to go through life's struggles and disappointments, without the need to drink alcohol or use drugs. I thought how I understood and respected their consistent, disciplined manner of living each day.

Then I suddenly realized something extraordinary: It was not too late for me to show my parents that I could be the type of daughter they always expected me to be. I can make my footprints *alongside their footprints*. Instead of following in their footprints, I can actually make those joyful footprints with them now—in the present. This became a whole new incentive for me to continue to fight, and not drown in my self-pity with the devastation of the divorce. I knew reconciliation would be a whole other cycle with my ex-husband, because he has a unique intelligent way of approaching recovery, as he is a loyal doer of the 12 Steps of Recovery for approximately five years.

Through realizing how powerful the vicodin addiction was over my life, and to accept the sincere fact that I needed help, I finally believed that there could be a solution. Before you can attain hope for a better way of living, you first have to believe in solutions. Although if you do not acknowledge that you have a real problem, such as an addiction, you will not learn of any real solution.

This thinking came from my subconscious thinking I reserved from having attended A.A. and N.A. meetings over the last five years.

So I pondered what my next recovery trial would be. I remembered someone passing a business card to me while I was attending an outside A.A. meeting with my Illinois rehab peers.

As I glanced down and looked at the psychiatrist's name, softly running my index finger upon the bold black engraving, I contemplated on calling a person with the name "Griffin" that was printed on the business card. Although I hesitated on how Dr. Griffin would feel about me leaving the Illinois rehab before my 28 days were up, it did not stop me from calling. As

I contemplated the strong and yet humble presentation of his name upon his business card, I was re-encouraged that he just may be the one who will understand why I had to leave the Illinois rehab, having not recovered from my opioid addiction.

In my mind I pictured Griffin to be a wise, aggressive and yet empathetic psychiatrist. I began to believe that I already knew he would be what I have always needed in a doctor. It's a funny thing, but after having worked in a printing company that made business cards for Fortune 500 companies such as General Electric to the struggling sole proprietors, I gained a peculiar insight into the character of a person by how he or she appeared on their business card. Well, my premonition about the person, Griffin, turned out to be worth a call and worth saving my life.

I believed Griffin would have the patience to journey back in time with me to listen to how it all began, and who would then help me to finally understand myself enough to manifest our visits into a life of sober living.

In order to prevent him from developing a weak premature impression of me, I decided to provide him with helpful information about my good points, as well as my bad points. So, after leaving him an initial phone message, I wrote a supplemental email outlining a simple history of my recovery attempts.

In my email I described my past addiction-recovery psychiatric visits with my husband by my side, on to my 28-day stay at a Florida rehab center, while concurrently attending local A.A. and N.A. meetings where I was blessed to meet a genuinely caring sponsor. I brought him up to date to my latest trials with the Illinois rehab, explaining my reasons for failing to complete the Program. I did not want to overwhelm him with my alcoholic and drug addictive past, so I limited my email to the latest and the deadliest battles against the opioid addiction.

I informed him that I was on Suboxone, under a medical doctor's care that was licensed to administer Suboxone, an opioid medication blocker that would cause me to become ill if I were to fall back and take any form of opioid. I figured that if he knew the doctor's name and that my addiction was being medically monitored, it would add to the seriousness of my decision to want help to remain free of my opioid dependency. Along with the Suboxone treatment, I informed him that I re-entered the A.A. program on a regular basis, as well as church fellowship group meetings for positive influences.

I then added to my email, a short character profile of myself, including that I was a reporter for awhile after receiving a Masters Degree in Journalism from Columbia College. The last paragraph of my email introduction included the reason I wanted to visit with him. I told him that I wanted to sincerely *figure out the core issues for why I ever drank or used in the first place; to understand my addictive nature; and then to hopefully find the solutions to living an alcohol and drug free life.*

I was now on my own. After only six years of marriage, my husband finalized a divorce against me. I gave him no fight at all, because I never believed in divorce due to my faith in God and what the Bible says about the covenant of marriage. I was entirely against going to court—it was simply way out of my character to look upon my loved one in a court room to end something that is not suppose to end until death do us part. He claimed that he could no longer support me in my fight for sobriety, among other co-dependencies that he felt were only bringing chaos into our marriage. He filed for divorce approximately eight months prior to my admittance into the Illinois rehab. Although he halted proceedings pending the outcome of the rehab, he then resumed full force after I left the Program.

So the following year, he presented me with the "Dissolution of Marriage" documentation stamped by a divorce judge on May 20, 2009, which just so happened to be my birthday. If he would have waited only four months, perhaps he would have been able to accompany me to meet the doctors whom God placed in my life to resolve me from the addiction. But I was already out of "our" or more appropriately "his" home and on my own, moving into different apartments trying to survive.

But I never gave up on my faith in God and the light that burned within my soul as a conviction against my involvements with any mind-altering substances. So with the support of Dr. Dora Dixie and Dr. Griffin, I would make it to become a whole woman—actually for the first time in my life!

Eventually if you are truly committed to the 12 Steps of A.A. and N.A., you will want to help others who are fighting the alcohol and drug battles. I am only beginning to help others, but it is my prayer that God grants me the opportunities to repay enormous portions of compassion that were so graciously bestowed upon me through A.A. and N.A. meetings—in most recent through psychiatric one-on-one meetings—through encouraging talks with my family—through the Assembly of God Church—through my best treasure of private reading meditation time in my *Life Recovery Bible*.

Despite the actions my husband took, I tried to accept that it was something he needed to do for his own peace of mind. He did try to help me for five years, so I had to always remember to be grateful for the time that he did stay by my side. I had to forgive him for divorcing me, but that would come in the action of an A.A. step I had yet to climb.

Although seeing Dr. Griffin was not going to change the hands of time and bring my husband back, I knew I had to do this for myself and for others who needed me. I felt hopeful as I pushed the "send" button on my computer to let the introductory email message go to Dr. Griffin. I felt I did the right thing with preparing Griffin with my background, prior to our first session. I was confident that his business card impressed me with the right instincts.

While I waited to hear from Dr. Griffin, I attended an A.A. meeting with a new disposition—a new frame of mind and spirit. It was not like before when I walked into meetings and just *played along*. I had attained a new respect for the 12 Steps of A.A. and N.A. This meeting would be different. I would reverently profess among my peers my commitment to Step 1—that I now recognize I am powerless over my addiction.

Previously I would go to an A.A. meeting with the phobia of running into people I had partied with in the neighborhood bars. I would be scared of what I would say or how I would react. Now, during this recovery interval between Illinois rehab's departure, Dr. Dora Dixie's intervention and Dr. Griffin's hopeful prospects, I suddenly lost the anxiety of seeing former partying friends—the fear just disappeared. It was completely gone from my mind. It was as far from my thoughts, as the earth from the sky. It was a good feeling and for once in my life, I was building a real confidence that I could soon live as God willed for me to live. I trusted God was preparing me and helping me to overcome my fears, because He knew *my need for sobriety now blended with my desire for sobriety*.

I attended the A.A. meeting in full disclosure that prepared me to be completely honest for my upcoming one-on-one visit with Dr. Griffin. I knew that the honesty was fundamental in my healing, and that I no longer could hide behind any defensive thoughts that deceived me from seeing my life as it truly existed. Furthermore, by attending the A.A. and N.A. meetings as I waited to hear from Griffin, I knew that I would encourage him to trust in me that I was serious about my recovery.

So as I continued to attend meetings as I patiently waited for the "good doctor" to call, I had time to consider what I expected from the doctor. I jotted notes and various points that were important for me to discuss with him. I analyzed how I wanted the doctor to help me, whereas in the past I never took the time to prepare for such matters.

I needed him to reach out to me in a special way. I needed that favored treatment, especially knowing that my life had drastically been complicated from being happily married to being divorced. I would be suffering new anxieties now that I no longer had my husband by my side. I wanted to address each and every issue, because I was looking for healing at any cost and would do whatever it took to attain a joyful status—living God's way wholly, and not just half way.

The A.A. and N.A. meetings I attended as I waited on the doctor's sessions helped me to regain my self-esteem. I recognized that I am not obligated to please others as I have in the past. Just like that, I awoke to a realization that had me spellbound for so long. I could never displease anyone even if it meant harm to myself, which was perhaps a great trigger to my self-abuse. Suddenly, I was looking at myself from the outside and realizing core reasons for why I felt a need to drink or to use drugs, and I began to journal these observations into a notebook that I intended to share with Griffin.

I started to lose the guilt that would formerly engulf me if I did not respond immediately to someone's request. I was not harassing myself any longer with what everyone else thought of me. For the first time, I was placing my needs and goals first.

After three days had passed since my email was sent to Griffin, I was finally called and invited to come in for my first two-hour session to begin at 11:00 am through to 1 pm. It was the perfect time session to travel to his office located in the Chicago Loop. I was excited and hopeful. *The first thing I would admit is that I am on Step One of the A.A. and N.A. Program.* This would be a mutual solid starting point!

The night prior to my first visit with Griffin, I slept better than I had in months. I was sincerely looking forward to doing this for me—and not for my husband. I know now that if you try to recover for someone else's benefit, it just will not work. Recovery will only work if you want to do it for yourself. It is a simple statement but a profound action.

The next morning as I waited on the "el" train platform, I reassured myself about the visit that would soon manifest: "This is good," I said to myself. "I can't wait to share with the doctor what I self-analyzed . . . . to start with some positive stuff . . . that just may keep me coming back."

Straddling across the morning traffic of downtown Chicago to the doctor's office, my confidence was bursting. I was seeing the glimpses of joyful living to come. It was a good feeling. I thanked God for blessing me with this new opportunity. I knew this was an awakening time in my life between Illinois rehab and

Dr. Griffin . . . I was truly recognizing my present addiction and past addictions with a true desire for resolve. For the first time, in the deepest part of my being, *I was on Step 1 of the A.A. and N.A. Program: I admit I am powerless over alcohol and drugs—that my life had become unmanageable.*

Step Two

WE CAME TO BELIEVE THAT A POWER GREATER THAN OURSELVES COULD RESTORE US TO SANITY.

"My thoughts are nothing like your thoughts," says the Lord. And my ways are far beyond anything you could imagine. For just as the heavens are higher than the earth, so my ways are higher than your ways and my thoughts higher than your thoughts.

(Isaiah 55:8-9) Life Recovery Bible

I will re-commit in front of Griffin, as I have already done so in front of my A.A. and N.A. fellow members, that I submit to Step 2 of A.A., and sincerely proclaim that I trust that God the Father through Jesus Christ is the Higher Power in my life that can restore me to sanity. I have reached Step 2 and am in reliance completely on God to make me whole again without turning to the carnal abusive addictions overwhelmingly available in the world. I do not want any of it; and only want to go forward to walking from Step 2 and onward . . . to truly live life on life's terms.

My life now means living in accountability to the 12 Steps of Recovery, and to continue to be a true example of one who is living the 12 Steps of Recovery, by working the A.A. and N.A.

Program and working the one-on-one therapy sessions with Griffin.

I am sitting comfortably in jeans and sweatshirt on a windy wet September morning awaiting the company of my new friend, my new confidant—a psychiatrist named Griffin who is going to resolve my chaotic past as to why I would ever desire to be drunk or high on drugs; that is, why was I born with an addictive personality . . . did my environment have something to do with my addictions?

I am relaxed and prepared for a calm session as I stretch my legs beneath the long oak table that supports a pleasant comfort zone of speaker and listener space. I reverently cross my hands atop the table, and in a concentrated serious-minded demeanor attempt to emphasize the importance of eye contact between me and my doctor that encourages an environment where an understanding of our reasons for being in this particular room at this particular time resonates.

Griffin looks at me compassionately and asks:

"How are you today?"

Griffin seems to truly care as he asks me how I am doing. For some reason, it does not come across as just an ice breaker. Although I am sitting four feet down the path of an exhaustingly varnished wooden table, I feel a bit closer to him.

Jan:

"Did you get my email?"

Griffin:

"Yes, I did. Thank you. It was a considerate effort on your part to give me helpful information in order to get to know you a bit and what you have been through. Yeah, actually I made a copy in case we want to review it together."

Jan:

"First, due to an order I must keep with our sessions and out of duly concern to reach my goal with our sessions, I want to verbally re-commit to Step 2 of the Recovery Program. Thank you Griffin. I want to re-commit or initially commit to each Step of Recovery progressively at each of our sessions. I need you to provide feedback to me as to how I am achieving the 12 Steps of Recovery. I need your honest analysis and feedback in order for me to know that I am following the Steps and fulfilling my duty to the Steps. I want to add your guidance tools from our meetings into my toolbox of sober living, along with the sobriety tools I have already attained up to this point in my life. I think it is important that we both understand the purpose of our meetings—to secure the 12 Steps of Recovery in my daily living, in part by flagging down the triggers to my using and replacing them with healthy manners of approaching life to strengthen my sober living."

Griffin:

"Yes. So, let's do soul searching as the Steps require us to do. And when we are done, I feel assured you will be living a life re-committing daily to the 12 Steps of Recovery."

Jan:

"Thank you Griffin, for agreeing to uphold this order of purpose to our meetings. It is important to me. I need this personal feedback from you that is difficult to attain during the A.A. and N.A. meetings. People listen at the meetings, but unless it is a special discussion-type of meeting, the norm is not to give feedback. People generally take turns one by one talking about how they are doing in their recovery, but I need to know from you, as we go forward, that I am personally living the Steps."

Then, to not waste a second of my precious time, I began my story—surprisingly about my sugar addiction at the age of four. I changed the structure of my story—instead of analyzing my latest addiction and going backwards to where it began—I went in reverse—from my earliest addiction to the present . . . perhaps I was more eager to get at the core reasons of why I began nurturing an addictive personality. I was on the clock, and I was determined to get real answers out of each session. My agenda was to go through each Step of Recovery with Griffin, and to have his assurance that I was carrying out the Steps with total commitment.

I now believed that the Steps and my obedience to God would gain me a sober life and some kind of resolve to why I ever relied on any substances to get through life. So I set the tone and order for how our sessions would proceed. I explained to Griffin that I would analyze my addictions and/or addictive behaviors in a chronological order, along with going through the Steps in a chronological order. The doctor appeared a bit confused, but did confirm that he was "trekking" with me, and commented that it may be a good experimental approach for his future recovery therapy sessions. He softly smiled that I received as my cue to begin.

Jan:

"I began eating granulated sugar straight out of the box around the age of four, and would continue to do this until I could walk to the store and buy candy. So around six years of age, I began eating excessive amounts of penny candy—where friends would mock me as they recognized my intake to be enormously greater than any of their candy rituals. Everyday I celebrated bags of candy and chocolate ice cream with friends, but could not help but notice that *I seemed to be the one who needed* the treats versus my friends who just enjoyed the treats. Some of these friends even saved the treats for the next day; whereas I could never save candy for the next day.

"I was bumping my head at night to go to sleep since I was about six months old. So, although the sugar would be my first addiction, I wanted to make the distinction that there was an earlier obsessive behavioral disorder prior to the sugar obsession. I felt it important to lay it all out—concerned that the more information that I give you, Griffin, about me, could only help in understanding if perhaps my obsessive behaviors may have led to my addictive behaviors. I did read and learn from the testimonies of others, that obsessive disorders are triggers to developing drug or alcohol addictions.

"So up to the age of about eight years old, I displayed an outwardly behavioral disorder of bumping my head each night, eventually submersing myself in eating granulated sugar out of the box. The sugar addiction would continue to grammar school by overly supplying my school uniform pockets with way too much candy. I believe it was M&M candies that were my first addictive candy. I ate sometimes up to six bags of M&M candies per day. I did not feel right about this. It is as if I knew this was not proper eating behavior.

"Early on, I realized there was something abnormal in my sweet intake compared to my friends. I also felt immediate remorse when I wronged someone or disobeyed my parents. As far back as my memory permits me to go of being a child, I seemed to have a guardian angel or perhaps it was the Holy Spirit of God that made me aware when my behaviors were not pleasing to God. As far back as my memory permits me to go, I believed in God, and that He had created me, and that He wanted me to live according to the commandments that He passed to His servant Moses as told in the Bible.

"Since I was four or five of years, I remember getting lost in a huge coffee table top white leather covered Bible that my father kept from Grandmother's funeral ceremony, and it contained the most beautiful drawings of Old Testament heroes for God, and of New Testament pictures of the Son of God, Christ Jesus. I always believed God was love and that His love surrounded me. I always felt it was my obligation as a little girl to rub the hands of the elderly people who suffered from arthritis. I would approach these people as they sat on their porches alone that I felt had pain, and just asked them if I could do anything to help ease their sufferings. They liked when I sat with them to just keep them company, and some who felt more comfortable with me, would permit me to rub their hands that ached with arthritis. These early good deeds I did as an adolescent made me feel good and helped me to heal the feelings about behaviors that I carried out that were unpleasing to God.

"God's first intervention of love for me helped me to survive a particularly difficult trial on my very first day of the first grade. I was an overly excited and overly talkative student; perhaps because I was one of the few students in the class that did not previously know the other kids through kindergarten. Most of my first grade classmates had attended kindergarten together and already knew each other. My parents decided that I would begin school in the first grade; and so I had many new friends to make. I was punished and called to stand in front of the class with my face to the blackboard for about a half of an hour for talking 'out of order.' Then if that was not enough to embarrass me in front of 30 or so classmates I did not know, the teacher told me to place the gum that I was chewing behind my ear and she told me to leave it there until the end of the school day.

"I think I may have been aware that chewing gum was breaking a rule; so at the tender age of six, I expected some sort of reprimanding, but I trusted my 'grown-up' teacher to know how to properly reprimand students. I could still see the frightful look in her face to this day when she admitted that she forgot that the gum was placed behind my ear, and therefore apologized for causing me pain through the whole day. After class was dismissed, she made me stay afterwards as she struggled to untangle the gum from the hair area behind my ear; until I permitted her to take the scissors and just cut whatever hair was obstructed by the sticky gum. Although the classmates knew I had to wear the gum behind my ear in my hair, they had no idea of the suffering that I would endure undeservingly after class was over. Everyone including the teacher seemed to forget that I was wearing the gum, except me. I have no recollection of ever talking about the incident with fellow students after that day.

"The teacher realized she went beyond her disciplinary authority in punishing me; and although she later apologized to my parents, the humiliation was unintentionally embedded in my soul *and did diminish my self-esteem.* It was the most exciting day of my little life—I was so excited to wear my red checker dress with its black pant-n-leather belt on my very first day of school. I can still smell the wonderful fresh cotton from my new clothing, and the fresh suede from the new school shoes that my mother had let me pick out over the weekend before school began. For my day to go from *this high peak of utter joy to this low peak of utter shame would affect my self-appreciation, my self-worth and love for myself, later affecting me to make poor choices beginning as an adolescent.*

"Later that evening, my father came off from his usual afternoon shift that he worked from 3 pm to midnight; but instead of ritually watching the midnight news, he woke me up to hear my story of the sad events surrounding my first day of school. He even put the bed side light on, which he never did, to see how much of my hair had been damaged by the teacher's poor choice of punishment, and he became quite upset. I remember telling him how I was announcing and singing the alphabet along with other students as the teacher led us. And to my surprise, the teacher told me that I was participating out of turn. And once I sat back down after facing the blackboard as punishment, she immediately reprimanded me again for the gum chewing.

"I did explain to my dad that she was sorry; but that was not enough for my dad, and he made sure that he took the appropriate steps for my first grade teacher to be duly reprimanded.

"He cried and held me in his arms as he flushed his fingers through my butchered hair that was gruesomely uneven on the side of my head where the gum was removed.

"The next morning he pursued disciplinary measures with the school's pastor, principal, as well as the neighborhood precinct captain in hopes that my first-grade teacher would be appropriately corrected for her somewhat abusive punishment to his daughter. *This probably was my first feeling of low self-esteem, and damaging enough to make a lasting impact.* I could not blame my father for being protective of me. I was glad for that, but I still felt ashamed and confused as to why I was the student to be picked on . . . . as there would be more prejudicial treatments to come, at least up through the sixth grade.

"It seemed that the parish, which was supported predominately by Polish families, was prejudiced against me for being of southern culture on my father's side; although I was proud of my last name, later researching it to be an affluent English name when I traveled to London, England. My father's background was English, Irish, and American Indian. I will never understand why I was never given fair treatment as the other students, who were predominately of Polish origin. The church and school were founded and built by Polish immigrants; so it is not that I did not respect the cultural and architectural talents of these people; but I just felt less favored in particular by the nuns, than the children of more impressive or unique international backgrounds. My grandfather on my mother's side was of Croatian origin, as he came to America in the late 1930s. But I never bothered to tell anyone, since I was bright enough to already understand that I had somehow been 'labeled.'

"And there also was different treatment to those children who were parishioners of the church versus non-parishioners of the church. I knew my parents were not parishioners of the church, and perhaps that had something to do with it. Most of my fellow classmates were of Polish origin and were from families who contributed the minimum offerings into the church collection baskets each Sunday that discounted their upcoming quarterly tuition fees. This was a favored arrangement by the parish leaders and school administration staff.

"Later when we entered junior high, my parents joined the church as parishioners, and then I noticed that my older sister and I were treated somewhat more fairly. So perhaps it was not so much prejudicial reactions, but rather favoritism toward the families who went along with the parish's preferences to receive tuition payments in the church basket that offset school budget operations. To this day, I can only assume what made me an unpopular pupil.

"Between first grade and tenth grade, I excelled in academics and athletics, but continued to suffer low self-esteem. Quite often I was moved with my desk in the corridor outside of the classrooms during elementary school, or into classroom cloakrooms with just a chair as punishment for talking out of order. It did not matter whether it was a nun or a lay teacher, neither hesitated to separate me from the other students.

"Neither the school's counselors, faculty or my family were aware that I suffered with ADD (Attention Deficit Disorder) and ADHD (Attention Deficit Hyperactivity Disorder), and thus the reason for my over-active and over-talkative nature.

"Despite the somewhat cruel or harassing punishment that went on for several years in grade school, it was in my spiritual nature to forgive those who picked on me. Too bad it was yet too early in time for the research that diagnosed medication for focus inability and hyperactivity (ADD and ADHD) to be founded. Presently I discovered since going through public school fellowship testing to be certified as a special education teacher that ADD and ADHD students are now given special consideration. Understandably, I was not officially diagnosed with ADD and ADHD until my late 30s when I began seeing my first counselor for addiction recovery.

"When I look back, I unintentionally permitted these childhood abusive treatments to demolish my self-esteem. But not to the point where I did not continue to try to regain self-confidence by keeping straight A's on my report card, and becoming the cheerleading captain and volleyball captain in junior high. These continued efforts did keep me out of trouble and helped me to feel more proud of both my father's background and my mother's background. Even if I was not always proud of myself; I never stopped loving my parents and my sister, and was grateful for how much they tried to protect me.

"As a freshman in high school I was on the starting string of an Illinois state championship volleyball team. I remember when we won the state championship the principal gave the whole high school a day off from school. This is a pretty cool memory. For awhile I was your average good high school student jock until I neared the end of second year high school, and then I would be confronted by a far more dangerous addiction than chocolate—something of a white substance known as PCP.

"After falling into bad company with teenagers who were going astray, I reached out for help at a friend's home bible study, and joined a few others in committing my life to Christ through a special prayer where I asked Jesus Christ to save me from self destruction and to renew my love for Him and His followers; thus becoming 'born again.' Upon becoming spiritually transformed by sincerely placing my faith in New Testament scripture passages during this Bible gathering, I received Christ as my Personal Savior at the age of 17, and became deathly afraid to ever go near PCP or users of such drug substances again.

"I could not believe how ugly I looked in a certain photo that I was shown by my sister, who had suspected at the time that I was under the influence of something stronger than alcohol or marijuana. This photo reinforced my diligence to take the narrow path of righteousness and to stick close to those people who prefer the ways of God versus the ways of wickedness that leads unfortunate souls to sin and death.

"I was so sorry to come to the realization of how I must have worried my parents and my only sister, who was two years older, who constantly watched over me, as she would re-commit herself to me repeatedly: 'You are my little sister and my only sister, so I must look after you.' I believe that God made my older sister my guardian angel during this time and up to this present day. The Lord intervened in love for the second time in my life when he saved me from PCP destruction. Yes, the Lord was working miracles in my life.

"During the summer of 1981, after finishing day camp counseling for my sixth consecutive summer, I was attacked by a man that wanted to rape me. Fortunately I was completely sober, and able to get away from his hold on me. He brought me to his apartment telling me that his wife wanted me to babysit. When I got there, she was not in sight. She fled with the baby and left him. I later found out that he was a psychopath, and again, God came to me in that dark gloomy apartment where I was almost strangled by this demonic stranger that I thought was a trustworthy person, and rescued me. This was my third intervention of love by God I consider to be my third miracle from God. My perpetrator was committed to an insane asylum and then died shortly later. I am just grateful that I was sober and walking in God's path when he attempted to physically injure me. I was saved by Christ, and I professed my faith in Christ and I was being obedient to God. I testify that God our Lord protects you when you are obedient to Him. I profess this to as many people who will listen to me when I am in group meetings, whether A.A. or church oriented fellowship with other friends, to this present day.

"I knew that God was more powerful than any drug could have over my life, and He abolished Satan out of my life. I made progress during my senior high school year by beginning after-school college courses, joining the National Honor Society, and attaining a part-time job as a health club aerobics instructress. Looking back, I can honestly say that I was turning to the first three steps of A.A., even though I had not yet been introduced to the A.A. program.

"I believe A.A. makes perfect common sense for those persons who are attracted to its wisdom and who willingly react by going forward to each successive Step. If you do not fully submit to the Twelve Steps progressively and repeatedly, you will fail, as I learned the hard way. Now I was already carrying out the start of the Program, but as is the unfortunate situation of many, I fell quite a lot before I was willing to move forward and to climb each Step of A.A. Therefore more addictive trials would befall my life. But then again, it would be a long time yet before I was introduced to how A.A. works, and thereby, truly give my full attention to the testimonies of those whose lives were saved by the A.A. Program.

"So later I would learn that I suffered A.D.D. (Attention Deficit Disorder), as well as A.D.H.D. (Attention Deficit Hyperactivity Disorder). This may have caused me to bump my head from infantry to eight years of age. Since such disorders were not recognized during this time, I was repeatedly written up on report cards as an intelligent student but too distractive to the class. Each year was the same evaluation, but my parents were never given any counseling advice because there was little if any proven research on such disorders common among children."

Griffin takes a quick note, and makes eye contact to be assured it's OK for him to take his turn, after seeing that I was sobbing upon my shirt sleeve. I came to observe since seeing various psychologists that it is wise they permit us, their clients, to talk as much as needed in order to open up our wounds of a painful past. Griffin knew with one wrong look or wrong sigh, let alone verbal element, he could completely shut me down . . . and the crucial moment is gone forever. He was good—he knew therapy—he listened well.

Griffin:

"So can I note that your first drug addiction was PCP?"

Jan:

"Yes, that would be the first drug addiction. As far back as the teenage years, there may not have been an A.A. group that I was aware of, so I needed to make that verbal commitment in front of believers in Christ that I wanted Him to rescue me and to allow Him to take control over my life. And that is what I did at the age of 17 at my friend's bible study. I knew I could not control my indulgences and that I was in desperate need of God's intervention and His guidance."

Griffin:

"I would also like to note that we have discovered the FIRST CORE REASON for your drug abuse. *That core reason will be documented as low self-esteem.* We must make sure that we not lose concentration of the core reasons that we discover behind your need to escape through substance abuse in varying types. Our ultimate goal toward your recovery *is that we rid you of these core reasons causing your sufferings, and need to cope by artificial substances that are destructive temporary band-aids—not healing band-aids.* These are sufferings that we must completely rid out of your whole being. Once we build your self-confidence and self-esteem, *your people-pleasing and other vulnerabilities that make your life less productive will slowly demise.*

"The ADD and the ADHD are mental distractions that you were born with, and must be given attention as existing mental core reasons for your substance abuse. *So, I am adding these mental disorders as core reasons along with the low self-esteem.* We first need to get them all out on the table, and then we will address how these can be coped with in a healthy way; which I am proud to say you have already begun the healing by the counseling you are doing, and by the group sessions you are now attending. You are continuously reaching out, and that is very good. I tell you this to enhance your self-esteem. I understand your intentions to be: that you want ultimate healing and to sincerely try to not let anything slip by our therapy that could creep up on you later and possibly tempt you into using again.

"We made a lot of progress; and I think this would be a good stopping point. I see something different in you that I have never seen in other addict patients. You were beginning the Twelve Steps before you even knew there were the Twelve Steps of Alcoholic or Narcotic Anonymous. Even though we will see later that you entered into other addictions, you remained strong from an adolescent onward in your faith and conviction in God. This is why you are still healthy, and fortunately in pretty good shape. God has saved you over and over. I know you have a purpose, and we are going to be sure that your confidence rises to the level of wanting to carry out the purpose that God has planned for you.

"You never really hit rock bottom because you were working the Steps of A.A. even before you were aware of their existence. You did not wait until you lost it all *before admitting you were out of control.* You came to believe that only God could rescue you from these mind-altering drugs that were controlling your behavior and hurting your family. And although you did submit for some time to God controlling your life, you slipped back into the abyss of addiction because you simply were not knowledgeable of the A.A. meetings and the vital 12 Steps of Recovery *in order to retain sobriety* and to stay away from falling back into further alcohol or drug experimenting. You did not have the protection you needed. That was not your fault. You need to know this. You were not given the tools you needed to stop after the first addiction. But we will be sure you have your tools now and that you use these tools daily as we progress in our therapy sessions. Don't you worry—now you will have the protection you need on the therapy end that will be encouraged by your unrelenting faith.

"I like that observation about you, and I want to see you in two days. We will do two sessions per week, and then eventually we will go down to one per week, and then one per month for as long as you feel you need my counsel as well as my support. We will go through at least one Step of Recovery, sometimes combining Steps, during each session. I believe we will work on Step 3 and onward through our next sessions. I believe you are committed already to Steps 1—3; and as we go through our upcoming sessions, you will be committing and achieving how to live all 12 Steps of Recovery daily in your life—that is, re-committing to the Steps daily in your walk of sobriety. So think about Step 3 for the next session and in accordance to your group discussions during your weekly A.A. and N.A. meetings.

"For now do not be concerned with addressing insurance issues with my receptionist Meagan today; just be sure she records our next appointment for 11:00 am. She will email you later for the insurance information so it does not intrude on our session time."

I see Griffin as my mentor, my counselor, my sponsor, and my friend; and I give him a warm smile of appreciation as he walks out of the room. We have an understanding. I leave the office already feeling secure and lighter, and *almost* as if I am glad to be me.

I am no longer in fear of the control that vicodin had over my life. When you are addicted to vicodin, you are no less or no more than "a junkie." It was the scariest time of my life. Running to pawn shops to get the money to pay $5 per pill going street price. Think about the waste of money when you are doing 10-15 pills per day at that cost! It is true that addicts turn into the most self-centered people, because they are most concerned with avoiding the pains of withdrawal. Although I did not steal from others, I stole from myself, i.e., from my health and my future.

Step Three

MADE A DECISION TO TURN OUR WILL AND OUR LIVES OVER TO THE CARE OF GOD AS WE UNDERSTOOD HIM.

Then Jesus said, "Come to me, all of you who are weary and carry heavy burdens, and I will give you rest. Take my yoke upon you. Let me teach you, because I am humble and gentle at heart, and you will find rest for your souls.

(Matthew 11:28-29) Life Recovery Bible

Prior to my next morning session with Griffin, I made a knee bent plea to God at my bedside: "Lord, Father God, I am now ready to turn my will and my life over to your control; please Father God, be my mind, my body, and soul—I give you my entire being as I commit to Step 3 of the A.A. Program. I make this commitment in the name of my Lord and Savior Jesus Christ. Amen."

I awake excited to begin my second session with Griffin. As I sit waiting for him to walk in to our private meeting room, the table today does not appear to be as long as it did during the last session. I think to myself: perhaps a symbol of our relationship becoming closer.

An appropriately two minutes past the 11 o'clock hour, he walked in the room dressed in a faded pair of jeans with a colorful sports jacket that stylishly revealed an attitude of confidence, not arrogance—I was impressed.

Jan:

"I meant to ask you last time if you did not mind that I refer to you as Griffin—I mean no disrespect, it makes me more relaxed when approaching you with the more personal matters of my past. Be honest . . . do you mind?"

Griffin:

"Hey, anything that makes you feel more comfortable also does the same for me. Anyhow, I kind of like it myself."

I graciously place my head face-down across my out-stretched right forearm while releasing whispers and groans as I am softly speaking, but with enough volume that Griffin will hear every word. I look over my arm to notice that Griffin has moved his body closer to express sincere interest to hear what I am telling. He also outstretches his arms in a folding manner as if he wants to show me that he is reaching out to me. I am not talking but just whispering softly and desperately to myself . . . and to my doctor.

Jan:

"Why was I never afraid to put down my nose or throat an unknown substance composed of a toxic chemical that would burn my right nostril while slowly diminishing the use of my cognitive and motor faculties? I was either decrepit in 'street smarts' or didn't give a hoot about myself. It scares me so to think back on the disturbed and irresponsible people that I hung around with in my past who established networks in dealing such drugs."

Images form into recognizable shapes as I disengage my mind, and my eyes naturally reflex to close. I am comfortable to be just silent in my own thoughts while in Griffin's presence. I now feel I am within my domain to set whatever mode or tone that will bring me to my past without the intrusive thoughts of the present. I feel we have an understanding that invites me into a comfort zone. In his own way, Griffin reassures my respite solitude for emotional release, by gently whispering for my ears only:

Griffin:

"Go back . . . what do you see? Can you share? Speak softly . . . or just recline to your own memories within your mind . . . . it is OK . . . ."

So that is what I do . . . . I share thoughts . . . . some verbalized . . . . some just thinking . . . but somehow I feel Griffin is able to fill in the blanks . . . . it is just a bond we are forming . . . . sort of telepathic . . . . so what comes to mind is:

"I am at a backyard party on a warm summer night, and a friend tells me: 'Did you ever try cocaine? It's way different than PCP. You will have control over this and it will not make you lose control of your mind, but just make you feel great.' Then a montage of flashbacks in many different locations with many different faces plays back to times of socially using cocaine and doing shots of Rumplemintz, Goldschlogger, Yagermeister, Ouizo, and Komokozi while singing kereoke.

"I see myself at various bars, house parties, and restaurant parties, gaining popularity through spending money on dinners, alcohol

and drugs with many different friends. I see myself with various boyfriends in lustful attractive interactions. There are no flashbacks resembling true love or quality sober dates.

"Then I fast forward to nights with a man who would become a long term boyfriend, and the first person I began to depend on in a unique way compared to any former relationships I have had in the past. This person is someone not easy to disengage from my memory, because although we fall out of an intimate relationship, many years follow with us doing this co-dependent partying weekend bliss to talk and to also enjoy social activities. We become each other's release from our family problems and rescue from friends, we feel, who have treated us unjustly.

"As time goes on, I begin to consider Herm to be a complacent and reliant person in my life to always be able to lean on despite the abusive arguments. He feels the same. So we retain our friendship for years after the intimacy is in the past. Although, I thought of marrying him in order to try to make things right with God. As I said earlier, I remained convicted by God's Holy Spirit to control my life since I was a very young child. But marriage did not seem to be favorable for reasons I would just like to leave out of the story.

"We have developed a co-pendency toward each other, and enjoy partying more by ourselves than with a group of other people. Both of us have grown out of the bar scene; anyway, that is something that resided as a strong denominator underlying our relationship. Even though I knew we were immorally behaving by partying on mind altering substances, mostly cocaine, that went against my faith, I did attempt to make things right. We did other activities to get ourselves out of the party scene, like going to museums and movies.

"If a life crisis emerged in his life, his so-called friends were never around. So I felt that is something hurtful, but yet real, that we both suffered. Perhaps he too, behaved as I did, because he had suffered low self-esteem like myself. I felt that Herm and I had a lot in common, but due to the constant arguing while we later cohabitated for about three years, I knew we simply could not become husband and wife in accordance with God's covenant of marriage.

"Even though I was trying to develop inside church relationships more, and even dating other men, I could not seem to shake the co-dependency that emerged in mine and Herm's relationship. My need to please Herm, my family, and other so-called friends, continued to grow stronger. It begins to take a toll on my life. My low self-esteem had emerged into the need to constantly please others. I was overly concerned with people-pleasing to the point of giving people money for their habits. The people-pleasing goes way back. I believe people-pleasing can be an outlet for good people who suffer low self-esteem and co-dependencies in sometimes numerous relationships.

"So, I continue to fight my morale regressions by keeping up with church, and being honest among prayer group members and within Bible study groups, that I need help. My fellowship in Christ and nonstop belief in my faith that Christ will save me, eventually takes me away from the party scene of bars and with Herm to a Christian husband I end up meeting at a Christian singles recreational event.

"We made a covenant of marriage with God at a Christian church on September 20 of 2003, the same year I received my Masters degree in Journalism from Columbia College, a ceremony that was attended by my husband and my family. I had to let the past go and move on . . . .but at this point I was backsliding again from my commitment to God by excessive beer drinking. I was also beginning to feel the creeping upon me of vicodin addiction at the beginning of my marriage. So I was ready at this time to begin becoming more *educated about recovery groups through church, and of course, through the A.A. and N.A. 12 Steps of Recovery. But I know now it would not work, because I was trying to please my husband, instead of being totally committed to pleasing God."*

Griffin:

"OK, let's stop there. *Now we must note the two (2) other core reasons: people-pleasing and co-dependency.* These, Jan, are quite popular core reasons why people become addicts."

Jan:

"Yeah, I know that now. I would want others to have a 'good time' even when I did not care about getting high. As I began disliking cocaine because of the paranoid side effect, I would just stick to having a few beers. But then the beers became addictive. That is why I earlier said, I was living half of my life submitted to God, but not fully . . . that is why I must confess by entire submission to you now that I am ready to fully climb Step 3 and continue to climb the Steps without holding back as our sessions go forward.

"Also, I want to note for us to bring up later that I believe I was co-dependent with my family way before I was co-dependent with Herm. I constantly wanted to please them and be sure that everyone was receiving the attention that they needed. For example, I would feel a need to take my mother out a lot because dad was working nights. Herm would help me to take my mother out during the times I was spending with him.

"Then I felt a need to help my dad with work projects, such as copyrighting his songs that he wrote or attaining patens for his inventions that he was working on . . . that involved a certain intelligence level for research. My dad had not been able to complete school back in Tennessee due to being a family provider at the age of ten years old. I feel sometimes the beer helped me to cope with my co-dependencies that at times were overbearing. Then I was also caretaking for my Aunt Jean who needed someone to help her to get out of the apartments she was living at, where the landlords were too strict on her, and taking her entire Social Security income. I made sure she would get a proper phone and a proper bed, and many more essentials she had never had living alone. I consider these not of co-dependency actions. Although it could be stressful being a caretaker and a full time worker, someone had to help her, and I felt God placed this ministry upon me. So I considered it a blessing from God, and will always consider it a blessing. I now understand better how my father felt the calling from God to take care of many more in his family. My husband helped me with family obligations especially concerning Aunt Jean.

"Finally, just to get everything out on the table for dissecting later, I now believe I became addicted to vicodin before marrying my husband, in part, to stop drinking beer. In my stinking thinking I believed that doing vicodin was not as unhealthy as drinking beer. So, as I said earlier, once you are in the A.A. and/or N.A. Program, you must constantly re-commit to the 12 Steps every day. You never give up. Perhaps you may fall, but you must get right back to Step 1, and never give up all the way to Step 12. It is an every day—take a minute—to an hour—to a day—to a week—at a time process. That is how it works with me, and how others have professed that it worked for them, also vulnerable addictive types as myself. It is good to know that A.A. always welcomes you back, even if you fall and need to start all over again. You come back to the meeting and re-profess your commitment and start taking it day by day again.

"Eventually when I met my husband, and became married, I was the happiest I had ever been in my life. Although I was taking vicodin, that started with a prescription for dental oral surgery pain. I could feel me becoming addicted, but due to my husband's love for me, I actually began turning to treatment for the first time. I was honest with my husband about my fear of addiction due to past behaviors. I also was honest with the addiction counselors.

"I will always be grateful for what he did for my family in the early years of our marriage.

"I was a reporter using my MS degree in Journalism in the beginning of our marriage, and doing well. But when I did not get a full time career with a prominent news organization, I took on some harsh jobs unrelated to my skills and expertise. For example, I was a phone technician and phone operator for a printing company in the suburbs during the last year of my marriage. Working 10 hours per day brought me quite a lot of extra income accumulated from time-and-a-half overtime payment succumbing to approximately $50,000 after one year.

"I was trying to make my husband proud, since my previous journalism work never paid that much. I really wanted to please my husband by contributing to the household expenses. Instead I did the opposite—I displeased him. Although in his defense, I did need to take medication for my ADD for the first time to get through high pressure jobs. He knew I was now abusing the adderall on top of the vicodin. For the first time, I just could not handle multi-level and highly-demanding jobs without help for my ADD. I had previously worked for good companies and for long times, but never on a stress level that was to come with the jobs I underwent while I was married.

"We had bought a home that needed a lot of repair, so I truly thought I could finally do my part to make a difference in the progress of our future.

"So ironically, the stress of pleasing the suburban company by working 10 hour shifts with no breaks, and pleasing my husband by seeking counseling from addiction psychologists and healing groups from church to stop using vicodin, I started to abuse adderall. I was feeling an even greater demand to use the adderall to make it through each day. I was honest at my A.A. meetings professing that I had drug addictions to vicodin and adderall. Although, my main concern of the abuse was the vicodin.

"I thought I could never give both of these drugs up at the same time. But guess what . . . I did. My full recovery would come, but a bit too late to save my marriage. I just could not seem to fulfill an agenda that my husband was demanding of me. But I never stopped trying, even after he abandoned me through his divorce of me. I continued as I lived in changing apartments, feeling completely alone, to fight my addictions that were affecting the demise of my life functions. And I also was convicted by God, even to a more critical affect through attending A.A. and N.A. meetings and truly listening to the testimonies of the members.

"Addictive-natured people have much difficulty taking medication *as prescribed*, (for example, the adderall). So that is why I fell back from Step 3. So although I was seeking counseling with my husband to the extent of going to in-stay rehab centers, I was still not fully turning my life over to God. I was not fully submitting to God. I was still too stubborn, and I just knew that I was not following the Program with the efforts that are needed in order for the Program to work. My husband grew intolerant and inpatient, and just wanted out of it all. So what was I to do to save the marriage? He wanted me to move out of the house, and gave up the fight with me as a partner. That hurt, because he knew my efforts were progressing. He had his own addictive behaviors that he was committed to resolving: so to handle all that confronted our marriage became too much for him. I understood that we needed to separate in order to heal, but I was encouraging him to not go to the ungodly level of divorce.

"As we go through the Steps, I think it is good to note that I am not only being healed of addictions, but more importantly, I want to be healed of the core reasons that underlined my first addiction to the most recent addiction. From my meetings through A.A. and N.A., I come to realize that when we address our inner demons or compulsive behaviors then we can truly fight the past addictions, and more importantly, prevent any new addictions from emerging in our future.

"So in conclusion, I want to find healthy resolves by gaining better self-esteem, and preventing any co-dependency behaviors from developing in my future life. I feel we can meet these goals, Griffin, I really do.

"I also recognize the isolation that vicodin and adderall commenced my life into, and now by trying to make better meetings, be it in church or in A.A. or N.A. meetings, I am confronting the isolation and trying to overcome that type of destructive life style. I am recognizing the isolation as a bad way of life, even if I am productive in my isolation, such as writing this book; it still is not good to cut off the rest of the world. Socializing with God-centered stable people is vital to maintain sobriety. And you cannot expect friends to keep calling, have pity on you, and be able to read your needs in some clairvoyant manner. You must reach out and continue to reach out, until you have a workable social life that detracts you from that comfort zone of isolation.

"You must forget the self-pity and stop blaming anyone else for your predicament—that is only behaving selfishly. And to stop being an addict means to stop being selfish, to face your fears, and eliminate the anger within—stop placing blame, shame or guilt on anyone other than yourself. This is my right way of thinking that I must reinforce in my daily awakening through prayer and meditation.

"I now finally recognize that I am the sole blame for my using—I made the decision to try to make my life easier by using, but it only resulted in making my life more difficult later. This is a general outcome for many addicts that I observed through testimonies in my A.A. and N.A. meetings, as well as church-related recovery meetings.

"Now just to fast forward with my latest addiction cures, I was cleaned from vicodin AND adderall 100 percent of January 2010. The Suboxone medication blocks any vicodin you may slip and take from having any europhoric effect on you. If you take a vicodin while on Suboxone, your system will become off-balanced, and you become scared to take any vicodin while on the Suboxone. This was the beginning of my abolishment to vicodin forever. God blessed me further by simply taking away the adderall medicine need just like that. The fear that resulted from the vicodin addiction had a chain reaction to the adderall and therefore scared me into stopping both narcotics. Yes, I additionally stopped 3-4 years of high adderall daily dosages 'cold turkey.'

"I now wear a medical bracelet with the engraving to alert paramedics and doctors to NOT administer vicodin to me if I am in any type of accident. I wear my medical bracelet as I now type these pages of my testimony. I also included on the same bracelet that I cannot be given adderall.

"Considering that my husband was not around to celebrate my recovery from vicodin and adderall as he promised he would be, I fell into a deep depression. But I never fell back into the addictions.

"The opioid addiction was absolutely the most devastating and painful of any addiction I had ever suffered. I know the pain of awaking to sweating and aching from the withdrawal of your body not receiving the opioid sustainment. The vicodin withdrawals were worse than the adderall withdrawals; but both just as harmful.

"I suffered several anxiety attacks due to the devastation of the divorce, So doctors from emergency room events prescribed good medication to help me cope with severe nervousness. But I never abused my anxiety medication. True commitment to the Program and to God has maintained my proper prescription in-take.

"My husband was supposed to begin marriage counseling with me. A pastor of Chicago's New Life Church advised him to take me out once per week to see if we can work things out. This was after I was clean. But he did not follow through. I was already into my third move within one year from apartment to apartment due to the high level of anxiety I suffered in the awakening to the deceit my husband had unintentionally placed on me. He may have meant well, and could not help his change of disposition due to his own personal intrusions or reasons, but what I expected and waited for . . . never happened with him. So I went into a third apartment, after losing a lot of money on prematurely leaving the last building via the lease rules, and began a summer of torture. I could not believe that I became aware that I did not even know the man that I married.

"But many would fall back into addiction after such disappointment. But thanks to my new Christian friend, Sharon Brown, who I found living across the street from me, thanks to the Central Assembly of God Church, and to the A.A. and N.A. Programs, I stuck with my sobriety. I am so proud that I did not allow his rejection of me to take me into another abyss of addiction.

"So, with the recommendations of psychologists and psychiatrists I have seen since Dr. Dora Dixie placed me on the Suboxone, such as you, Griffin, I have followed recommendations to discontinue relying on my former husband for any help in my future.

"I actually love him enough to this day to just hope that he is working on his addictions that I would rather not reveal in this book. His addictions are not the purpose of this book—it is a testimonial account of me, Jan, overcoming my addictions, and how I continue to do so.

"Now that I have lived alone for almost two years up to the time this book is published, and see that I have thus been unintentionally deceived, I am ready to face a new reality.

"He said the divorce was only a separation, and that the divorce paper meant nothing. I believed in him. He told me it was only going to be a separation. Well, he protects his consciousness with a different perspective. He will combat me by explaining it a whole different way. And I learned to accept that he has a right to see things in his reality as he does. But I know my reality is in check with doctors like you, Griffin, and pastors, like Steve Rust of the First Baptist Church of Chicago. This happened to be a new pastor that I met before completing this book that has helped me tremendously through trauma and depression that divorce havocs on one's life. Pastor Steve Rust and his beautiful spouse, Susan, lead a new church that I also attend here on the south side of Chicago.

"I admit I was wrong to be the first to say the word 'divorce' to my husband within our home, when I was angry to learn that he too had issues that I was unaware of . . . . .while I was truthful to him about my issues. I immediately apologized each time, and told him that I never want to really divorce him. I told him each time that I was just angry and truly sorry for using that awful 'D' word. Especially, when he was closer and closer to closing the deal with his lawyer, I begged him to drop the divorce. But once I came home from withdrawing my 28 days from the Illinois rehab for reasons previously mentioned, he sealed the deal with his lawyer, and the judge stamped the 'Dissolution of Marriage' documentation on my 46th birthday. Soon after that, I was out of the house. I did not even care where I went; I just wanted him to have the peace he seemed to desperately need. As I earlier said, I moved prematurely to the lease boundaries, so that is evidence that I was in no condition, mentally, to choose a good place to live. My first place was between Archer Ave. and Interstate 55. Living between two major expressways drove me out of my mind. The dirt and the noise that flocked over my living quarters everyday were horrible. My cat was so scared. I had no idea what I was doing. So now I live on Carpenter Street, and that was a much better decision for my cat. I at least have a backyard and a quieter area, considering my nervous condition.

"I had to let him do what he needed to do, and I had to go. And I have still no reconciliation activities in progress with him to this present day. He claims he simply is not ready. Oh well, that is how life goes. And I must take life on life's terms. No drugs will cover this up, as I learned now so vividly from past drug cover-ups. The reason I bring this up is to encourage any reader who is suffering from addiction, that if you have turmoil in your life complicating your addiction, it only gets better as you get more sober. The more sober you become, the longer you are sober, the more you can say 'bring it on.' The more you see your turmoils as trials from God to make you stronger.

"I did start smoking since the devastation of first hearing that he filed for divorce, but I have already re-applied my commitments to the 12 Steps of Recovery to rid my addiction of cigarettes, and I am succeeding. I have quit 'cold turkey' and fell back on some of my really down days, but I never stop trying to live my life without relying on cigarettes to ease my anxieties. The meetings and prayer help me to keep that cigarette from being lit.

"I am not blaming my husband for my wrong choice such as starting to smoke cigarettes since the abandonment by him, but I was so devastated by the betrayal, even if he did not mean it, that it would take a whole other book to explain further. So, Griffin, I hope seeing you can actually encourage me to stop smoking now, along with my church fellowship and A.A. /N.A. support.

"I have given myself to God and His way and purpose for my life. I have reached and climbed Step 3; yet I know I need to re-do every Step everyday, because I am not perfect. I still am healing everyday! So I want to go forward and do each Step repeatedly in my life. I want your help Griffin so I do not enable my core reasons, whether mental or physical to ignite any addictive behaviors now or in the future.

"Griffin, today, I am finally proud and honest to claim that I am not taking any medication for my ADD or ADHD, and it has been difficult, for example to concentrate and focus to complete this book. As far as the anxiety, I rely on reaching out to Christian friends, especially my sister, Julia, and my new friend, Sharon. Sharon truly reveals my shortcomings when I look at how much energy and dedication she bestows upon her elderly ill mother. She has helped me to be more submissive to God because I see that is the only way she made it through her hard times. So I want to be submissive in the same manner, to not only help myself to make it through, but to help others as I am helping myself.

"Her mother needs such delicate care, to the extreme that Sharon has to pull out certain ingredients from foods or vegetables so that her mother does not become ill. Sharon has to shop for special cereals like Cream of Wheat or Rice Puffs. She never complained not once to me in all the days I have observed her take care of her mother. Sometimes she has to leave church early because her mother needs her to help her to the bathroom. Sharon recently lost her husband who died young, and suddenly of a heart attack. So for me to see this young woman in her prime of life, give her life so lovingly to her mother's well being, only to cut her time for her bible study and worship with God's church, makes me stronger in overcoming my shortcomings. She makes me complain less about being abandoned by my husband, and she makes me want to do more for others. I truly believe that by serving others is the way to lose your self-pity and self-centeredness and selfish ways to live a more joyful sober life. So I am grateful that God brought Sharon into my life to help me through the 12 Steps of Recovery by being an example of a sober God-loving friend. And Sharon's good deeds go beyond that of her household, she also extends her services to other elderly in the neighborhood with any extra time that she has free while her mother rests. Once she asked me to get her mother liver from the store because it was something she needed to specially cook for her mother's diet, and I felt good to give her my service. This is how it works Griffin. This is the rainbow that is reached at the top and the rainbow you shall keep seeing if you give of yourself as the Program is constructed to be properly followed. I see it more and more clearly each day and through different people, because this is where my eyes and heart now lead me. I look more for God in people and the doings of others than the worldly fun that was so temporary and so easily forgotten in my youth.

"I have also reached out to talk with others who have encouraged me that I can make myself a stronger individual. Milica Trutin, my landlady has a strong ethical outlook on life. She has been a new role model to me. She had many trials coming to America as a immigrant from Croatia, but faced every trial to her success, without ever taking drugs or drinking. A new friend, Nona, of the Central Assembly of God Church, is my grievance group leader, and she truly cares about others. She is encouraging me to reach out to help others more to get out of my self-pity.

"As I would also like to disclose a new chronic physical ailment I began suffering with that is a 'woman's physical problem' that naturally would cause any women severe depression. I just want to disclose everything that could be triggers for me to fall back—but I am reversing their affect to make it all the stronger of a purpose that I become stronger, relying on God and His people, as my healing and comfort. If I get through an abandoning divorce and then a severe womanhood physical painful ailment without failing back, I want to express the power that God brings upon those who are serious to put His ministry first. I am doing physical therapy which is difficult, but with the work and the fellowship, it helps to make the day go by and since it's a productive day, it helps you to sleep through the night. And the best is that you awake to no remorse or regret for how you handled your day. You immediately pray to our God to help you in the same way for every hour of the next day."

I slowly bring my head up to meet Griffin's eyes to give him the body language that I am now ready for him to say something.

Griffin makes some notes in his journal and rises to pose an invite:

"Well our time is up to day, but I will see you at our next appointment, and we will chart out your core reasons and all your past addictions, to understand how they relate. We will eventually arrive at solutions to convert your chronic personality shortcomings into healthy defenses—something you had not examined in the past. Drugs are unacceptable to you now—you want a stronger perspective on your self and how you relate to others and to situations that will make it natural for you, finally, to enjoy your life. Come on partner, let's walk to the parking lot."

As we walk together to Griffin's car, the wind is picking up. The fall weather brings in early darkness, and it is sort of refreshing from the exhausting hot long daylight hours of summer. I like this guy because I know he is becoming a friend. He does not cut me off just because the scheduled time is up.

Jan:

"I do not want to forget to examine genetics along with the ADD and ADHD, for physical core reasons. I am not sure if my parents or any relatives have ADD or ADHD.

"I did have an aunt on my mother's side that was an alcoholic and died of cirrhosis of the liver at the age of 47. I just don't want to forget to contribute any family background information that you should know as we include analyzing my physical core reasons that contributed to my developing an addictive nature.

"And when you construct your chart, you may want to indicate that a few family members on my father's side suffered chronic mental nervous breakdowns beginning when I was a young child. No fault of anyone's, but this may have contributed to my lower self-esteem. Sometimes some of my disabled family members would be made fun of in the neighborhood. You know how people could be cruel to others of this nature? I do not want to go too far into detail, because the subject is me and not any of my family members. Although my husband reflected upon my family's dysfunction relating to my drug abuse abyss, similarly, it does not serve the purpose of my book to expand upon my husband's lectures to me. I know I am not unique in family dysfunction affecting one's self-esteem. I just am thinking of anything that may help you and me, Griffin, figure out what may have affected me to not love myself enough to hurt myself intentionally with my former drug and alcohol abusive mannerisms."

Griffin:

"That is good, Jan! Right now you need to let your husband go completely. For the most part, you also need to let your family go completely. We will only concentrate on you—you're healing, you're reaching all the Steps of Recovery, and you're continuing to follow the Steps of Recovery every day in your life!

"It is important that you continue your hospital doctors' visits and the church group sessions to uplift you from your depression. It appears to me that you have always given support to others all your life. Well, now it is your turn to only, and I mean only, think and act for 'Jan.'"

Griffin expresses the importance of what I am feeling, and congratulates me for making progress. I am pleased with the time we spent. As we depart—me to the train depot, and him to his car, I graciously extend a hug and a kiss on the cheek . . . just felt a need to express my gratitude in a way that I was accustomed to doing with others. It was important for me to be assured that all was cool on the subjects we discussed. So when he comfortably accepted my gesture of appreciation, I got the reassurance that there was no need to feel guilty or weird over anything we talked about.

As I lay my arm outstretched on the window sill of the train, I flashback to stories my mother would tell me about how her and her twin sister, Jean, grew up with a father that was already 80 years of age when they were yet teenagers, and how he had taken them away from their mother.

I needed to reflect on how my parents' way of life as they grew up, may have some reflection on how I turned out. Not that I blame by parents for my wrong choices, but it is good to make those connections . . . . I think to sort of observe the whole environment of what was impressed upon me from my parents. Both Mom and Dad grew up in poverty and hardships that I am grateful to this day that they protected me and my sister from suffering.

I reflect upon a disheartening story that my mom told me that had always made me feel compassion for wanting to be a friend to her and her twin sister, my Aunt Jean.

One rainy evening, my mom Joan and Jean are lying in bed as young teenage sisters, when they hear their mother, Evelyn, trying to get inside their window from the outside. She is yelling at them to open the window. Before they could decide what to do, their father, John, comes rushing through the gateway on the outside of the house. They fearfully witnessed him yelling at their mother to leave his daughters alone. He scolds their only mother to get away from their house. Joan and Jean are crying as they hold each other in complete disarray to what they observed. They do not understand why they cannot live with their mother and father in the same house, as their classmates did. Mom and Aunt Jean never did have friends . . . just classmates. The situation at home not only affected their growing-up years, but would affect their social lives up to this present day.

I think back at the stories of my mother waiting for the Salvation Army to bring her and Jean clothing for them to wear to school. I think of their celebrated bakery treats they were so excited to enjoy with their dad when he received his social security check. Mom says her life was simple, but good and clean. She played with jacks and a rubber ball and hop scotch, while Jean sometimes jumped rope. They perhaps received a doll once per year from the Salvation Army that they would share. They were happy just to walk to the park and swing on the swings. This was a "high" enough for them. They never thought of the need to use drugs or drink. They saw teenagers drinking around them, but would not dare approach these sorts.

I am sort of envious, as to what gave my mother this innate ability to appreciate life and her family to that level. She said she would be too scared to take drugs and to hurt her body. This is just simple smarts.

I get it now. I just did not get it when I was 15 years of age up until now. But I get it now. Mother shared beautiful simple stories of growing up, and I would lay with her in bed before Dad came home from the midnight shift, and love to hear her stories of growing up. She did not look for boys. Her mother actually arranged for her to meet my father. It was an arranged date between her mother and my father's father Wilson. How sweet is that!

My mother tried to tell me do not chase boys and do not drink or do drugs just to please them. It is not attractive in a woman to take drugs or to get drunk. So, thank you Mom for trying to keep me on the right track. I am sorry I did not listen and truly take in what you tried to instill in me years earlier. But I get it now. I get it. I want to go back to her little house on the block of Princeton Avenue where she grew up and do Double Dutch jump rope with her and my aunt—but I cannot. That was not my time. So now I want to hurry to her to hear more stories. Now that I am sober, I want to hear the stories again. I want to be happy to just jump rope, and not with a beer sitting on the side of the steps. You know what I am talking about, those who like me, felt you needed a "high" to do anything. Why, did I have this innate wrongful need for a substance high to accompany my life's activities????

I know it did not innately come from my parents. So I will be sure this is ruled out with Griffin. Perhaps there could be relatives who may have been users or drinkers among my family circle, but definitely not my mother or father.

Noticing I still have another 15 minutes before my stop, I flashback to my father's hurtful stories about his family moving at least 15 times since he was a young boy working as a sharecropper with his father for different landowners, whom provided them living quarters in return for their labor.

Dad is working in cotton fields beginning at the age of 10, and unable to attend school regularly because he had to help his father provide desperately needed funding for his family to survive. They move continuously as they are hired by various farm owners to pick cotton, sow and harvest corn, or to milk cows on dairy farms. My father is a young boy on top of a tractor instilled with the drive to get the job done, because one day he will be trading in the tractor after saving enough funds to purchase a used car to drive to Chicago in hopes for a better job to support his family. His faith in God and his love for his family will make his dream become a reality. He sees his future, and it keeps him going.

He saves the quarter that he makes after a long day's work of moving cows from one pasture to another, not letting up for one moment on his dream that this type of hard labor will one day end.

As he watches his father picking the cotton and rubbing his aching back as he bends to be sure he is pulling the cotton according to the landowner's demands, my father's drive increases in determination. "Jimmie, pull that cotton, you know we get more money from pulled cotton over the picked cotton," yells his father from across the cotton field to his son.

Rose and Lil, the younger daughters are off walking to school in patched clothing that is clean and decent. Rose makes her own little room in the two room cabin house where eight family members lived by placing a curtain up to off-set her dressing area. She was "country"creative. She used a solid sturdy box for her own little dresser. How sweet. This gave her privacy that made her feel good as she grew into a teenager. She did not complain. She made things work. She just made things work out. She did not need a pill because she was angry that the family lived in a two-room cabin.

Jackie is outside climbing a tree as little Lil looks on; and they are happy to just have outdoor life to enjoy. They swim in a pond, or walk the railroad tracks, and this is fun enough. Sometimes they walk with their older brother Jimmie to get a coke and "moon pie"at the nearby country drug store. This is fun enough. There are bad boys around that they see stealing or up to no good, but they are simply smart to just stay away from that type of "fun."

Their brother Jimmie stays back to help but makes it to the country school house at lunch time to bring his sibling sisters baloney sandwiches. The sisters return home from school later that day to help their mother to sew and to clean house and to can jams and jellies. The next morning, Jimmie's mother Birtie makes fresh biscuits, and depending on how much money Jimmie and his dad were paid, she may be able to put some bacon in the biscuits, but more often the kids would have to settle for jam. Jimmie does not mind and neither do the other children. They find happiness in their life, as hard as it appears to be, they are happy.

The thought of altering mind substances is no where near their thoughts. Perhaps Jimmie may be thinking of seeing a picture show in town, if he gets Saturday work at the saw mill in another town, but these thoughts diminish when he can no longer keep his bicycle to ride to the saw mill to get the quarter to see the picture show.

Sometimes he walks the 10 miles or so there and back, but not as often as his bicycle permitted him to do.

The family is sitting in front of the fire at home eating popcorn and listening to Jimmie sing, and they are happy and fine with life. Birtie has made a beautiful quilt for the girls to sleep under, and Wilson has placed bricks on the barrel fireplace to warm so he could place them at the ends of the children's beds to keep them warmer at night.

No one is thinking of going to drink at a nearby bar. Life is clean and simple, even though it may be poverty stricken—the self-esteem and self-respect of each family member is not stricken.

I get off my stop and instead of being on a busy city street, I wished I was on a country road at night, walking home to sit by the fire with my dad back in his day. They were unaware of drugs—they did not need anything to make them feel good—the country was beautiful enough. I sort of wished I was born in an earlier time, but then I would not be the daughter of the parents I have, and that thought displeases me.

So I put myself back in the present and see the bar lights and the liquor signs, but ignore them and head home. They grew up with less temptation around them—unlike me. I think this is a fortunate element to their time and their way of life in the country, but I do not allow it to excuse my willingness to have partaken in any abusive alcohol drinking or drug using.

I am proud of my parents and aunts for dealing with situations in their lives that were much tougher than the situations that I have thus far had to deal with in my life. I am proud that they chose to live life on life's terms. Just having something to eat and something to wear to go to school were hardships for them. But they handled it all the way up to this very day.

Neither my parents nor my aunts (with exception of a great aunt) have ever deterred to relying on any artificial means of gratification to get them by. That is strength of character I want God and my parents to witness in me while I am still fortunate to have the opportunity to change. So I realize now that I have tough genes too! Those are the genes I am using now! This is a good motivation that takes me into my sleep for the night. Griffin is helping me to have hope.

Step Four

WE MADE A SEARCHING AND FEARLES MORAL INVENTORY OF OURSELVES.

I am not sorry that I sent that severe letter to you, though I was sorry at first, for I know it was painful to you for a little while. Now I am glad I sent it, not because it hurt you, but because the pain caused you to repent and change your ways. It was the kind of sorrow God wants his people to have, so you were not harmed by us in any way. For the kind of sorrow God wants us to experience leads us away from sin and results in salvation. There's no regret for that kind of sorrow. But worldly sorrow, which lacks repentance, results in spiritual death. Just see what this godly sorrow produced in you! Such earnestness, such concern to clear yourselves, such indignation, such alarm, such longing to see me, such zeal, and such a readiness to punish wrong. You showed that you have done everything necessary to make things right.

(2 Corinthians 7:8-11) Life Recovery Bible

Before I even sit down at Griffin's table, I cannot wait to let out the frustration I feel about my past way of behaving.

Jan:

"My eyes are now finally open to *how selfish an addict can be*. It is no wonder that the factor of fear plays such a significant negative impact on the former addict when he or she finally takes a moral inventory of what he or she has done to herself or himself, and loved ones while under the control of the substance. A new shortcoming immediately enters the inventory and that is *self-pity*. This needs to go. You will never get sober if you self-pity your life or blame others for your situation. So fear and self-pity will come probably around this Step 4, and I have already faced these elements in my meetings, and I now want to re-evaluate my moral inventory with you, Griffin.

"I was co-dependent sometimes on my parents to a level that did interfere with my marriage. I constantly wanted them to have fun that they did not have as youngsters. Sometimes I did vicodin just to escape the stress of trying to please everyone and keep them happy. So these were the first shortcomings I took a serious look at in my moral inventory. While I was on vicodin and still married, and heavily involved with my parents coming to our home for entertaining in various manners, it became concerning for my husband because he noticed that I was 'using' in order to keep up with the static or chaotic agenda of pleasing my family.

"My husband would say things such as: 'Jan, you should just let them live their lives themselves; you never know, they may be happier if you stepped back and sort of dissolved away from their social lives. My husband was not the first to say that I was co-dependent toward my father, my mother, and my aunt.

"Although Aunt Jean was not a co-dependent relationship . . . someone in the family had to step up and be Aunt Jean's caretaker once she became disabled. I became Aunt Jean's caretaker for housing and nursing aids, and proxy for various government aid matters necessary to her survival.

"My husband became frustrated with the obligations I volunteered to uphold for my aunt, and that somewhat impacted his decision to divorce me as well. In his defense, he felt I was using substances to overcome the many chores that came along with taking care of an elderly relative. He was wonderfully supportive in the beginning years of our marriage, and was even proud to do so. I remember him saying that it was his ministry from God to help my aunt. He once promised my aunt before we moved her into a senior housing complex that he would always be there for her. So when he discontinued supporting me with my family, I was shocked. I could not foresee this type of behavior unfolding from a man who claimed to love and serve God. But again, in his defense, I agree with him that I did use vicodin to falsely ease the stress of my obligations.

"My father's past history exemplifies a family that stuck together through poverty and hard times, and the siblings are still close today. I do not think of it as co-dependency, *but just love for family*. So where do you draw the line between co-dependency and acting out love for a family member?

"Grandpa Wilson had my dad sowing and harvesting corn during his adolescent years when he should have been going to school to learn to read and write.

"So, today, if I could help my dad in matters that he needed my higher education of writing to assist him, then that is what I did. For example, helping him to edit or copyright his Blues or Country music song lyrics or reviewing various paten applications for his latest inventions. As hobbies, my father is a songwriter and an inventor.

"Although Mom was quite smarter than me in many ways, and managed to be a great secretary to her number one boss, her husband James, and supported my father in everyway. Mom held respectful government jobs before her retirement, initially for the Veterans Administration and later for the Drug Enforcement Agency. She typed faster than 100 wpm—something I surely never did, but my sister would inherit that skill. I was fortunate to inherit some of my parents' natural skills: Mom's book sense, and Dad's writing skills, but I just never used these inheritances to their full potential due to my addictions. What I did not inherit was my parents' wisdom and "street sense" to stay away from abusing alcohol or drugs in order to remain healthy, and to stay organized in such matters as bank accounts and other financial events.

"So I had great leaders and great examples set before me, but refused to listen. My parents tried over and over to lead me on the right path. They always said I was too intelligent and too much of a good person to fall into such bad behaviors. Fortunately my sister did inherit their wisdom in this regard. So my sister was able to be my guardian angel. So despite my shortcomings, God still placed some sort of order in my immediate family to make my salvation plausible."

Griffin:

"I figure your main reasons for starting to use back when you were a teenager up through your life now are due to your having ADD and ADHD; you're genetic predisposition to drinking from your mother's side, i.e., her aunt; your low self-esteem; your co-dependency traits; and you're people-pleasing traits. And you may have been criticized in various ways of these weaknesses in your character, which caused you to become fearful of them. And thus fear becomes the overwhelming bad feeling that you want to escape. At first you were using to *cope* with the above character flaws, but as you became aware of your flaws throughout life, you made attempts to end these descriptions of your way of living—you became fearful of them.

"But fearing them is where you are at now! We, you and I, do not want you to fear these people-pleasing; co-dependency or ADD flaws—we want you to resolve them! Face them and cope with them, and do not hide behind them; because if you turn them into fear, it can, and has made matters worse for you.

"For example instead of drinking to deal with people-pleasing core defaults in your character—you needed vicodin—something worse and even more dangerous of an escape, to deal with the fear of people-pleasing.

"What do you think of my analysis on your predisposition and vulnerabilities to use; and how I have noticed that your use has progressed as you camouflaged your defects with scarier re-actions, such as fear? I know it sounds confusing. But you have been sincerely trying to rid yourself of your defects, but not facing them—just fearing them—which are antagonizing your personal growth in the Program. It is natural to be fearful when you first realize some defects of character that you had not realized before that hurts you, but then you have to get over the fear. Fear then is the next important element that we approach and confront when we reach Step 5 of the Program."

Jan:

"Wow. Griffin, that is exactly where I am now. Because now I am opening up honestly about my feelings and fears to others, outside of God. I am facing my fear through my church and A.A. and N.A. meetings. I agree and then some . . . I feel so much reassurance in how much you have paid attention not only to our personal talks, but to everything I have written in emails. Thank you for that . . . ."

Griffin:

"Now let's talk about the co-dependencies . . . when did you start feeling as if you were codependent to someone?"

Jan:

"It started with Herm . . . a boyfriend that I partied with and went out with to many places. We ended up living together but would fight too much. I knew we were not meant to be . . . because we ended up living together which placed me in constant conviction because the life style I was permitting went against my Christian-based morals . . . which caused me to escape my guilt by using even more.

"So it turned into an unhealthy relationship. We sort of blended more together to party . . . but that is as far as the relationship was going to go. I give Herm credit for at least always admitting that our relationship would not develop into anything more . . . he never gave me false hopes. He saw it as it was . . . and although he became co-dependent to me . . . he always told me that I deserved more in life than he could provide for me. He would be supportive of my leaving him at any time for someone who would be a better match for me, and have more in common with me."

Griffin:

"Well it is definitely easy to understand how you wanted to please him due to feeling somewhat of a responsibility toward him. It seems in your case, that people-pleasing and co-dependency were traits that kept you in a vicious cycle with Herm as well as other friends, and family members. When you have this constant need to feel that you must please everyone, well, that is enough of stress to cause already addictive-natured people to use in order to escape the overbearing stress.

"But now that you have acknowledged the damage that your personality weaknesses have caused toward your addictive nature, you are taking an awareness more often to not allow yourself to be the 'former Jan.' You are seeing the red flags go up when certain individuals may prey upon your good heartedness, and you are using your tools from church, from A.A. and N.A., and from our talks, to guard yourself from falling into old behaviors. You are becoming more active with individual initiatives to join church groups that serve your needs; and you are continuing to remain committed to the Program Steps of A.A. and N.A. You are on the right track. As you come and share your progress with me, we will be sure that you successfully climb each Step of Recovery, we will not stop our sessions until both you and I are sure that you are living the recovery steps on a daily basis."

Jan:

"I am so grateful to just have someone that seems to mold so perfectly with the desires of my healing in such a way that gives me a strong encouragement that I shall be victorious. Our sessions are a gift from God, as I see it, and my prayers are that we will see my sobriety to be moving forward in a progressive and sure-footed path, so that there will be no fear of ever falling back.

"Am I on the right track to feel obligated to take a personal moral inventory of my actions and possible invading weaknesses against my recovery every day?"

Griffin:

"Yes. You want to be as diligent in strengthening your sobriety by being on guard 24 hours a day, seven days a week, by re-committing to each Step. For our next session, we will approach Step 5, and do not concern yourself with too much information that can stress you and even cause you unnecessary anxieties. So, please for now, I want you to continue to re-commit to Steps One through Four, until you see me next time.

"In the A.A. and N.A. programs, there are specialized meetings for certain Steps. So if you can go to any specialized meetings that are focusing on Steps One through Four, that is what I advise you to do for now.

"Jan, I want to be not only your psychiatrist, but since you presently do not have an A.A. or N.A. sponsor, I am qualified from my various leadership involvements with the A.A. and N.A. Program, to be your sponsor.

"As a sponsor, we help to point our specifics of the A.A. and N.A. books that we feel those we sponsor should concentrate on as they move to each new Step. And we will cover and be sure that you have successfully succumbed to each Step and have sincerely committed to re-commit to each Step every day. Now that we have acknowledged your major inner core reasons for the plausibility to your using or escaping, we can flag the triggers that ignite these core reasons, and abolish them, on a daily basis, and your confidence will grow as your sobriety grows.

"This cannot be accomplished without a supportive network beyond our visits, which you seem to be putting in place. This is good. So our process shall be one that we take the Steps of sobriety together; so at our next meetings we shall analyze Step

5, Step 6, Step 7, and so forth. We must go through the Steps of Recovery during our sessions, and if you still need to see me after that, you shall."

Jan:

"Ok, I will review my A.A. and N.A. books prior to our next meeting along with my Life Recovery Bible, and make notes to prepare to successfully achieve Step 5. I think we are going on an organized and comprehensive approach to my healing and my protection to remain healed. Thanks Griffin, I'll see you soon!"

Step Five

WE ADMITTED TO GOD, TO OURSELVES, AND TO ANOTHER HUMAN BEING THE EXACT NATURE OF OUR WRONGS.

Even Gentiles, who do not have God's written law, show that they know his law when they instinctively obey it, even without having heard it. They demonstrate that God's law is written in their hearts, for their own conscience and thoughts either accuse them or tell them they are doing right. And this is the message I proclaim—that the day is coming when God, through Christ Jesus, will judge everyone's secret life.

(Romans 2:14-16) Life Recovery Bible.

Griffin and I had been keeping up with a twice weekly session to go through the Steps. Step Five brings a remembrance of my father telling me that he had to stop hanging around with special friends whom he cared deeply about. They were so good in so many ways. But they always had to revolve all their social activities around drinking. My father told me that it was very hard to stop going places with them, because he felt that he may have been "brushing" them off. But he was not. He was already in his sixties, and knew if he kept going their route of socializing, he would not be alive today. And now about ten years later, my father proves his judgment a smart call. Most of these former "buddies" of my father's are dead. It makes my father feel horrible to lose such good people to such a horrible disease. But it reinforced my father's decision to let them go. He had no choice. Their drinking was beyond normal, beyond socializing. They would get drunk, and depend on my father to get them home. So, he knew if he were going to live a longer life for his daughters, his wife, and his grandchild, that he had no choice but to give up the "fun times."

Unfortunately these friends of my father's could not go out without getting "blind drunk," and my father could go to the same places and just have a coke. Like today, my father takes my mother to the Blues music environments, but they drink coke, and they have fun—good natural fun. I envy that—but I am now inheriting his genes in an environmental way—even if I did not inherit them in a genetic way. Although I am paranoid to go into any bars, and will not go into a bar for several years now, even if my father asks of me, I know my boundaries and I abide by them. Best of all, my parents understand, and they only asked me once to go with them to hear Blues music, so I can hear my father sing. Once I declined and gave them my reason for it, they never asked me again.

Although this is understood between me and my parents, there is still an anger issue I bring up now and again with my parents. I must constantly ask God to forgive me for my "out of line" behavior.

As I am walking over to Griffin's office, I am thinking about a comment my dad made to me the other day: "Jan, you are angry at the world. That is your problem." It followed some negative discussion we had on personal matters that are not necessary to reveal in this book. But I had to check with Griffin to analyze if my fear had turned into anger. Now, if I am actually angry, and have wronged others with my anger, I want to tell that "third person" as it says in Step 5, that I over-reacted, and was wrong.

Griffin walks in while I am noting in my journal.

Griffin:

"Hey young lady, what are you so intensely writing about?"

Jan (for the first time I cannot help starting my words with tears):

"I want to change from now on toward anyone that I have previously taken my frustration out on . . . like my father. He told me recently that I was angry at the world—that because of the divorce, I was taking out my anger on others, such as him. Could this be true Griffin?"

Griffin slides the Kleenex box over with a sort of smart-butt reply:

"Come on, Jan. You should know this is the result of a healing addict from your meetings in the Program. Of course, you must go through an anger time, to succumb to healing. Anger and fear are two elements that must come forth and you must get rid of . . . in order to truly be living the Steps. If you do not carry out these emotions, then you are truly not living the Steps. So look at it in a positive way. The shorter you can cut it, the better for your opponents.

"You are very angry at your ex-husband. And now that you are sober, instead of 'using' to hide from your anger, you throw it out at someone such as your dad. You acknowledge this, and that is living Step 5. You know it is wrong, and you change. It is better for you to be aware of your anger at others, than to go back to 'using' to just hide behind it, and forget it.

"Fear and anger are so natural to be felt, so do not let it upset you—but when someone does not understand the phases of the Steps, they may get hurt. So you should explain to your father what you are going through. Even bring them to a meeting, your mom and dad, sometime. Perhaps an open speaker meeting from A.A. or N.A., so they could understand and appreciate why you may have had outbursts at them."

Jan:

"So as I graduate from Step 5 to Step 6, I must face my anger in positive outlets versus using substances or drinking. So again, as I must re-analyze my fears to overcome my defects, I must understand that my anger defect which is now more prevalent than ever because of the recent divorce my husband put on my life. I now must face this anger, but not by shaming and blaming my ex-husband for my addiction defects, but facing the anger against myself for formally permitting myself to allow anger to cause me to increase my substance use or drinking."

We make the session short that day, due to my horrible cramps that come upon me. I am going through this "change of life" and sometimes the cramps are simply too much to bear.

But as I wait for the "el," I intend to face fear and anger with Griffin during our future sessions, as we go forward through Steps 6 through 12. Griffin assured me before leaving that we can always review Steps, as we must re-commit to all the Steps every day of our lives. So reviewing any of the Steps with him in any of our sessions, is a good thing, he said to me. So I feel good about that. He promised that we did not have to be academic about it. Griffin explained to me that the Program of Recovery does not work like that—it is more of a leisure type of healing. When something is forgotten about during a previous conversation, it is OK to bring it up later, even if I have advanced to a new Step in our discussion.

Step Six

WE WERE ENTIRELY READY TO HAVE GOD REMOVE ALL THESE DEFECTS OF CHARACTER.

Those who belong to Christ Jesus have nailed the passions and desires of their sinful nature to his cross and crucified them there. Since we are living by the Spirit, let us follow the Spirit's leading in every part of our lives.

(Galations 5:24-25) Life Recovery Bible

The night prior to my meeting with Griffin where we will discuss Step Six, I sort out new defects that I find in my behavior that I want to discuss with Griffin. It's sort of funny, but as I play with my roommate, Samson, my cat of five years old, I sort of rehearse to him what I shall say the next day. Our playing goes well, and Samson is in a good mood. So I go to sleep that night with reassurance that I am ready for good or bad criticism from my trusted psychiatrist and friend.

For the first time, I am embarrassed as I am running late for my session. But I think with a box of Dunkin Donuts and two cups of Starbucks coffee, I am hoping Griffin is forgiving.

When Griffin sees me rushing and carrying the goodies, he smiles, and calms me down with a reassuring smile that lets me know that he is not upset that I have run late.

We both take a bite of the donuts and a good drink of our coffee together. My breath has slowed down a bit, and I feel I am ready to begin. Griffin is folding his hands nicely on top of the table, and this is one of his signs to me that he is ready to listen. It is sort of nice when you come to that level of knowing someone that makes it easy for you to talk. In the past, I have had few who were as compassionate and empathetic as Griffin. I thank God to myself in my thoughts for having Griffin at this time in my life. I begin to reflect on what Step Six now challenges me to in my present state of my life affairs.

Jan:

"I feel 'defected' now in different ways, prior to the vicodin, adderall and earlier addictions. Now there is depression, anxiety, fear, and anger that I pray everyday to God to take away from my behavior and interactions with others.

"My scars probably have never been as re-opened as they have since the divorce, but I confess these self-pity feelings to God everyday, and to others whom I trust in, and my re-dedication to the 12 Steps of Recovery help me to be kind, caring and sincere to the problems of others.

"I realize I am not the only one suffering with a devastating divorce, and I must realize that others need me to be strong to help them. I want God to use me through assignment requests from my pastors and sponsors. I am following instructions from my medical doctors for painful physical defects I now suffer. I follow instructions from my physical therapist for these physical ailments as well.

"I have already reached out in the church to be in a grievance group with women that have similar depressions, and I pray that I can one day be ready to help others so that I can get over myself.

"Even though you continue to resolve your former defects to why you began using, you must now take note of new defects that come out once you are sober. And Griffin, you are helping me with the fear, the anger, the depression and the anxiety. Just coming here puts these bad emotions in another place. But at night time, they tend to intrude upon my complacency. So I have books to read that I would like to show you. One of my pastors gave me a new book that is helping me with ridding myself of anger, fear, anxiety, grief, and depression. Once I am done reading this book I hope that I can pass it on to another who may be helped by it in the same way that it is helping me."

Griffin leans over to receive the book that I have brought for his opinion.

Griffin:

"*Walking Through the Valley of Depression and Grief* by Dr. Jack Schaap. Well, I have never read this book, but it does seem to fit the needs of your state of being at this time. I would suggest you read this book and others like it. Also, Jan, it would not hurt to join more groups besides the A.A. and the church group you are now in. You have been through a serious trauma immediately upon your recovering from two very difficult narcotics to overcome. You need as much self-help books as you can possibly make time to read. You need to continue talking with those who make you strong. People that have been through divorce and have made successful outcomes of their lives despite the hurt and the pain are good people for you to associate with—it can only help you."

Jan:

"I would like to stick to Christian groups and Christian friends, because of my faith. But what if I find a group that is not necessarily Christian, but still is helpful for those who have gone through the trauma of divorce?"

Griffin:

"Jan, you can join other groups if they help you in the emotions that you are suffering with, it is OK. At this time, you can make the Christian groups your priority, but I would not rule out other types of groups that could be extremely helpful. The more you mingle with others, the less isolated you will be. I feel you are still isolating yourself too much. And this allows nothing but more time to think of the past. You must let the past go, as hard as that is to do. You need to make yourself more busy, and continue to build your skills, so that you will be able to go back to work when you are more stronger."

Jan:

"Well, I do know that I can use more friends. My sister and Sharon, my friend from church, are busy with family matters, and do not have much time to socialize. So I have been looking on-line for building a richer friendship circle. I do go to the Christian sites, but have not been giving it the dedication that I should. I know that I need to talk to people at night more, when these ill shortcomings play upon my emotions in a harsh way. So I will promise to do better in this regard. Some of the A.A. and N.A. members are supportive to talk with, even though they are not from my church. But since I do not have a car, there are certain speaker meetings that I tend to miss that I would like to go to for encouragement."

Griffin:

"I think you are well enough to drive. So if you can find someone to help you to attain a good used car that would be a good investment for your sobriety growth. You should be attending more A.A. and N.A. meetings. I know some are far from where you are now living, but reach out more to people for rides. There may be people who are going to these meetings who live closer to you than you are aware of who can pick you up and take you home."

Jan:

"I agree. I have already given a used car purchase idea some thought. I was going to try to wait until after I move again so that I do not put too much new stress on me. I do not want any new stress at this early stage in my sobriety. Since I have only been sober for one year from the vicodin and the adderall, I am still so vulnerable. I know I will not fall back on these particular drugs ever again. I am scared to death of ever taking such dangerous substances, and still am amazed that my health is as good as it is after the abusing I have done to my body.

"But I feel that too much pressure, such as the co-dependency and the people-pleasing factors we have discussed earlier, could bring me back to relying on using to get me through commitments. That will just serve zero purpose in my recovery and make me a hypocrite to the Program. That is the only reason why I have gone slowly on my group selection and participation."

Griffin:

"That is wise thinking. So take it slowly, but I do want to see you make more progress in attending meetings. This is the only way to build strength to fight the past shortcomings and any possible new shortcomings that may intrude on your positive attitude. A positive outlook is so important for you, as a recovery addict, and for you to be a strong influence on your peers that you talk with.

"Has anyone who would formerly say you were too angry or too depressed say that they now see changes in your behavior?"

Jan:

"Some people have said that I have been much better in the last few months. They are proud that I no longer speak of the divorce. They are proud that I try to keep the conversation uplifted. I will call my friend Sharon to tell her about new things going on at the church, or I will ask her if she needs help with her ill mother. And she likes this, and she tells me thanks for helping her. This all makes it better for me to get through my day. I do have other friends too that have complimented me on my change of attitude.

"I must say I recently had some anger issues occur with my father. But I immediately notice what I am doing. I really search and inventory my behavior, and then ask my father for forgiveness.

"But my father commented that he cannot continue to keep forgiving me if I continue to take out my anger on him. This makes me sad because I know he is elderly, I could cause him dangerous stress because of my self-pity, and I do not want to be the reason for him falling into depression. He has had enough to deal with all his life as a caretaker of his family at such a young age. The last thing I want to do is to hurt him with words. Wounds from bad words are worse than wounds from knives. I know this Griffin, so I just have to stick to the Program and a positive outlook.

"So now instead of leaning on my father when I am feeling down, I call others that are younger and stronger. Although some do not have time to talk, I still try."

I cannot help the tears that begin to flow from my eyes. I break down and place my head upon my folded arms upon the table. I tried so hard to keep the tears back, but when I think of the outbursts that I placed upon my father and mother, it just tears me apart.

Now Griffin moves a bit closer to me at the table and places his hand upon my head. He tells me it is OK, just let it out Jan.

Griffin:

"It is OK to cry, and it is healthy to cry. This is the first time you have shared your love of your family in this way. I understand why you are in the pain of the divorce now. It is not just you that your spouse hurt; but because he hurt you, he also, perhaps hurt your family. This is how you see it. Am I right, Jan?"

Through his body language, Griffin emphasizes to me that he is somehow taking more of an interest in my recovery, and more so, a sincere caring in my recovery. This is so important to me, and I acknowledge it.

Jan:

"Yes Griffin. I am really hurt that my family has been hurt by the divorce. They celebrate my recovery, and then boom, they have to de-celebrate my marriage . . . if there is such a word. This is what tears me up. But what can we do or say. I have tried with my spouse to restore the marriage . . . and there is no point. You may have noticed I hate using the term: ex-husband. His last response was: 'I am not ready to reconcile.'"

Grffin:

"That is why we are going to stop right here and now with the husband. So how are you feeling about Step Six, and your success with it? What I want to know is how well is Step Six reinforcing your recovery?"

Jan:

"Well, there is some physical ailments that I must deal with that may or may not be a shortcoming involved with the drug abuse. But that is a 'woman issue' that I am handling at Loyola Hospital. And I am attending to that . . . but the weight gain is another shortcoming. So now I must not go back to my younger years of being addicted to sugar. Remember the sugar story?

"Since I noticed I gained weight, I have cut back on the sweet treats in which a lot of addicts begin to purge on, especially if they were once heroine or alcoholic addicts. I actually gained 20 pounds, but today noticed on the scale that I lost five pounds. So that is good. I feel it shows I am aware and defensive against those shortcomings that I must rid my life of . . . . beginning with the gumballs.

"For some reason, I started to begin an addiction to eating these large gumballs from the store vendors all over the city. I actually found myself taking the bus to restaurants or Dominicks grocery store, where they had these gumball machines in the area of the stores where you get your grocery carts.

"Well, now I kicked the gumballs. And believe me, that was not an easy task. But as encouragement to my readers, Griffin, of this book, that you are aware I am journaling to write, I want to encourage our former addicts or alcoholics that once you give up the worse of the poisons, the lesser poisons become easier and easier to give up. You begin to stop allowing any carnal substances of this world to ever bring you back into the abyss.

"As I spoke about with the divorce and the abandonment by my husband, I now see how these devastations have made me into a stronger woman than I had ever been in my life. I know I have to stop blaming him for his deceitfulness of the way he handled the divorce, because if I do not, then I am not recovering according to the Steps of Recovery. If I want to truly heal, I must stop discussing the divorce. This has been the hardest and most difficult of my shortcomings. The hurt has been the worse and most painful of anything I have had to overcome, and that includes the drug abuses. So if I can overcome the shortcoming of frustration and anger feelings regarding the divorce, then I know I am truly healing as the Steps guide us to do."

Griffin:

"Jan, you are getting there. You must be getting a lot out of attending the A.A. and N.A. meetings, as well as your church recovery meetings. Because, by golly, in my professional opinion, you are continuing to go the journey—and to go all the way'!"

Jan:

"I even apologized to my spouse for my wrongdoings, and he seems to have difficulties accepting my apologies. So now the best gift I can give him from my recovery is to leave him be in peace. And we will never repair, unless he too follows through the journey of the Steps as he should. He too must see his shortcomings. I have not yet witnessed that, and I will no longer concentrate on that. I am finally ready to go forward with my life, without him. I do not want to monitor his recoveries any longer—and I hope he will take no part in monitoring my sobriety any longer as well."

Griffin:

"We can actually cut this meeting a bit shorter, unless there is more you need to discuss. I like how you are letting the marriage go. And I believe you are sincere. So you go girl! And I'll see you the next session."

Jan:

"Thanks Griffin. Actually I am going to see my aunt today, and visit others to get out of myself. I look forward to doing more of this type of living. I want to escape the isolation, and bring other positive people who love me into focus. And I know this is the way to go.

"See ya later alligator!"

Griffin:

"Ok so watch your anger and your sweets, and hey, we will weigh you next time to see if you are doing good on the health end."

As I walk out the door, I give Griffin a wink of the eye, and I say an Amen to the Lord, and shut the door and suddenly think of how beautiful people can be when you are sober to see their true identities. God will reach out to you through so many others when you embrace humility to where God wants you to go. Tunya, my mail lady, who barely knew me during this past summer, offered me to come live in her home when she witnessed my depression from the divorce. I told her that I needed a friend to talk with sometimes as I sat in the yard alone. She reacted in such a caring manner to offer me her home for companionship. When you are tuned into the beauty of the people out there—it encourages you to keep going! I thought: What a beautiful soul. And how many more God will bless me to meet as I stay on His Path.

Step Seven

WE HUMBLY ASKED HIM TO REMOVE OUR SHORTCOMINGS.

Two men went to the Temple to pray. One was a Pharisee, and the other was a despised tax collector. The Pharisee stood by himself and prayed this prayer: 'I thank you, God, that I am not a sinner like everyone else. For I don't' cheat, I don't sin, and I don't commit adultery. I'm certainly not like that tax collector! I fast twice a week, and I give you a tenth of my income.' But the tax collector stood at a distance and dared not even lift his eyes to heaven as he prayed. Instead, he beat his chest in sorrow, saying, 'O God be merciful to me, for I am a sinner.' I tell you, this sinner, not the Pharisee, returned home justified before God. For those who exalt themselves, they will be humbled, and those who humble themselves will be exalted.' O God be merciful to me, for I am a sinner. I tell you, this sinner, not the Pharisee, returned home justified before God. For those who exalt they will be humbled, and those who humble themselves will be exalted."

(Luke 18:10-14) Life Recovery Bible

As I contemplated this Step 7 the night before seeing Griffin, I realized more than ever just how many shortcomings we all have outside of drug addiction faults. What is so refreshing about sobriety, is that you are more alert of how you react to others and to disruptive situations.

For example, friends that I thought were my friends never wanted to hear about my sufferings with the divorce abandonment. I always thought a friend would listen to you, and give empathy to your sufferings. But I found out that my former friends did not define the true definition of what a friend is. But I cannot condemn them for cutting me short, because I have no idea of the pain that they may be enduring in their lives at the same time that I am enduring this divorce abandonment in my life.

But I did conclude that true friends still somehow make time for each other and check up on each other, and will allow a friend hurting to talk about what is hurting that friend. Friends that I once shared with my husband, who did not want to hear about his divorcing me, I will not name in this book and I will forgive them. They are still sisters of mine through Christ. Whatever their reasons for not wanting to help me by letting me talk of my frustrations, is for their own reasons. So God brings new friends into my life. He brings me harvests of blessings just at the right time (Galations 6:8-10).

I found a super wonderful friend since the divorce abandonment, Sharon, and she is a member of the Central Assembly of God Church. I also found friends like Nona and Peggy through my special group meeting of single women through the Central Assembly of God Church as well. I also renewed my friendship with Kathy, an old friend of the Central Assembly of God Church. These people helped me make it through the hot long days of loneliness this past summer when I slowly had to realize that my husband was not coming back.

So God quickly takes away my rejection from other friends by replacing them with friends who have more in common with me, and therefore know exactly the kind of compassion and love that I need. I am grateful to Kathy, Nona, Peggy and Sharon, and I hope they read this book to know how grateful I am for them helping me to restore my life and to remain sober.

For example, even though Sharon must care 24-7 for her disabled mother of 88 years of age, every minute of the day, she still made time to listen to me, as I did to her. And the same for my other Central Assembly of God friends. So I had to mention them in my testimony of sobriety because they are a huge segment of the foundation of my sobriety and the new found joy in my life.

Sharon lost a husband to death four years earlier. Ricky, her beloved spouse of many years, and her first sweetheart died of a sudden heart attack. Ricky walked in God's path. This summer, both she and I, began talking. I would listen to her pain in how it is to lose someone that you considered a soul mate. Although I now know that my husband was not my soul mate, but Ricky was definitely Sharon's soul mate.

Sharon was someone that I admired and looked up to. Despite all her constant responsibilities for caretaking a very ill 88 year old mother, she still made time to listen to me, and to encourage me to get over my husband.

I love Sharon dearly, and am so grateful that God brought a true friend into my life at the dire time that I needed it. According to Galatians 6:9—"so let's not get tired of doing what is good; at just the right time we will reap a harvest of blessing if we don't give up."

Sharon and I would talk about our sorrows and losses, in between her monitoring her ill mother's diabetes and having to cook each meal to the upmost extreme detail carefully so her mother would not ingest harmful ingredients. I am so fortunate to not just meet another sister in Christ, but a true friend. I would help her in her sorrowful loss with her recently deceased husband, who died at the tender age of 49, understanding her immense pain. And although I was succumbed in my own whirl of emotional turmoil with the shocking turnout of my husband's abandonment to me, I would still sincerely try to help Sharon understand that God has more for her to do in this world.

One day she will understand why Ricky was taken away from her. That time will come. Until then, God has brought her closer to Him. Perhaps in my loss of marriage, God wanted to bring me closer to Him. These are the types of conversations we would have. Together, we made it through the summer of this past year in 2010. I know she considers me a true sister/friend in Christ, as I consider her. So I must appreciate this from God.

And I will get to that point, as I feel I am already getting there. God is showing me greater things in life—but it was a hard and scary road. But I see how sometimes God may put us on a narrow path to bring us back to where he wants us to be in our walk with Him. Books in the Bible such as the Book of Job, is a good example of how one's losses could be one's awakening to the blessing God has in store for them.

A friend of the name Kathy, I earlier mentioned, is another friend that I outreached to at the Central Assembly of God Church, as *a role model for woman's strength*. I see now how important it is to reach out to those who have survived difficult trials in life to strengthen my walk of sobriety. For example, Kathy, had to overcome severe difficulties with her health. She was always positive each time we talked even though she was in pain. She was consistently encouraging me that it will get easier. She has lived on her own almost all her life, and said she, as well as me, are not alone because we have God always surrounding us.

So I look forward now to what God has yet to show me, and to ask of me to do for His work to advance His kingdom. So I am becoming less and less afraid. And this coincides with the 12 Steps of Recovery. Faith is a huge factor in getting well, and becoming stronger and stronger as a soldier for Christ. Sharon and I both are learning this together. So I think our friendship is God-sent, God-anointed, and God-blessed. And Sharon, if you are reading this book, I want to personally thank you for being a true Christian friend to me, as the apostles were to each other during their tribulations.

I look forward to further growing in my faith, and am grateful to have a friend who works with me, and does not cut me off, but is soft and gentle, when I go astray. She has a gentle way of bringing me back to live on terms of the Scriptures, and you just cannot attain a better friend than that. Even when I offer her help with her mother, she is so humble to not want to impose on others who are suffering, but takes a little, perhaps a package of liver from the grocery store, that she permitted me to bring to help her in administering her mother's so careful proper diet. I am glad we are at that point to accept help from each other.

Before I could even get a positive word on how I was responding to the latest of the negative happenings, friends, I thought were friends, would just cut me off. But to truly be living in the

Steps of Recovery, you cannot let this harvest any new anger within you. So I am not allowing the latest of my rejections in phone calls from those who do not want to hear about the abandonment divorce linger any anger within me. Because then I am not overcoming shortcomings or character flaws. If I were to let mannerisms of others get me down, I may turn to cover up the rejection by "using."

But that will not happen. I came too far in changing my frame of character and way of approaching life and others. I want the best for them, and if I bother them, I must leave them in their own surroundings of their own issues.

When I come to Step 7, I think of all the wisdom that comes from the A.A. and N.A. Recovery Program, similar to the wisdom that comes from the Book of Proverbs in the Bible. If you read the Book of Proverbs, there is much wisdom you will wish you had used prior to "using." But that is OK, because the Book of Proverbs can still be quite a Godly supplement to your every Step of Recovery.

I am already sitting in Griffin's office, eager to share my observation of the wisdom of the Steps of the Recovery Program in relation to the wisdom in the Book of Proverbs. I want to re-commit today and everyday to Step 7, in order for me to be wise.

In order to recognize when you are being selfish or thoughtless of others' feelings, you can immediately rectify these matters with people, and it could make a world of difference. You can make good friends by being more knowledgeable of your shortcomings. Because what I learned from my A.A. and N.A. meetings is the more you seek change in your attitude and your personality, the more forgiving you are of the shortcomings of others. This is a recipe for good friends and a content life.

Two tenants that I came to befriend in my building where I presently live, Rosemary and Fred Barker, were angels brought to me by God *again* to keep me pushing forward. Although Rosemary and Fred discussed several conflicts in life they were confronted by, each time I ran into them I would never feel any anger or disappointment in their demeanors. They take each day as a blessing from God; so if you just open your mind to observe these positive reactions people maintain, you will soon pick up on their vibes. But you must be open minded and not wrapped up in yourself to observe the beautiful people that cross your path.

Griffin walks in and seems to be in a good mood:

"What's up Jan, how we doing today?"

Jan:

"I had some disappointing calls with friends of the past that were both friends of mine and my ex-husband. And I came to the conclusion, that it is probably best to leave these 'shared friends' out of my life for now.

"I think when you go through a really harsh divorce, it is better to make new friends. I have learned this through experience. I must realize not to be angry at friends who want to be neutral in the matters of discussion concerning my divorce. To me, that is my acknowledging my shortcomings. For example, today I apologized to a former friend that was a mutual friend of mine and my ex-husband, for cutting me off from speaking about my latest hurtful feelings from the divorce abandonment. I at first hung up on her for telling me: 'If you are going to talk about him or the divorce, then I don't want to hear it.' After thinking and praying for a minute, I immediately called her back to sincerely apologize, and to say that I would keep her out of it in the future. I must realize that she may be going through harsh times in her own life, and right now cannot handle any negative talk. And I am trying to understand that, even if I expected differently.

"So I feel good that I did the right thing to apologize and to just let it go. Since God gave me Sharon to talk to, and a few others in a special grievance group through the church; those are the friends and sisters in Christ that I will discuss my life and its downfalls as well as upfalls with . . . and be happy that God has given me new friends. And more importantly friends that are sisters in Christ."

Griffin:

'That is great Jan. Truly great progress! That you did not blame her for not wanting to talk about anything negative, and furthermore for giving her understanding as to why her position is as it remains. You are getting it. This is living Step 7. You are trying to immediately recognize your shortcomings and resolving them as soon as possible. As we never know what tomorrow may bring in any of our lives. And you do not need more regrets to add to your list of life-long regrets now. Although you believe you are forgiven by Christ, you must live the salvation of grace in gratefulness that Christ has bestowed upon you. Recognize your shortcomings, and rid them! For example, you do recognize your disagreements with your dad, and you are the first to apologize. That is good and humble. Being humble is the biggest character change of an addict's life style. And you got it! I believe it is engrained in your soul.

"Just keep going with that consciousness and humility for others outside of yourself."

Jan:

"That is why Griffin, I offer to help Sharon with shopping sometimes for her mother's very special diet. I also continue to take care of my aunt. I volunteer to help others on the block. And this is a true gift from God. You really have to get out of yourself, and your self-pity, to make it, to be stronger, and to not need a man, or a woman, to make your life complete and worthy in Christ.

"Ok, well I am off to my grievance group with the Central Assembly of God Church, and hoping to encourage my fellow sisters who are suffering as they struggle living alone as I do. This is where God put me, and I will make the most of it. I'll see you for Step 8—thanks so much doc!"

Griffin:

"You are more than welcome. And trust me, you are living the Steps. We must rid your anger for your ex-husband to truly let go, and have a free life to do God's Will. So our next session, be prepared, to rid your life of the marriage gossip. You may think I am hurting you, but I will not be as harsh as your former friends who just cut you off. To me, that was not the way to handle someone who went through the devastation and shock that you went through. So since I want to continue to be your friend, your counselor, and your sponsor, I will be a little gentler. See you then, sweetie!"

I cannot help myself. I run to give my friend, my counselor, my sponsor, my doctor, and my brother in Christ, a huge hug. Perhaps I needed the body contact comfort, but he was receiving of me. That warmed me emotionally through to the next session.

Step Eight

WE MADE A LIST OF ALL PERSONS WE HAD HARMED AND BECAME WILLING TO MAKE AMENDS TO THEM ALL.

Two people are better off than one, for they can help each other succeed. If one person falls, the other can reach out and help. But someone who falls alone is in real trouble. Likewise, two people lying close together can keep each other warm. But how can one be warm alone? A person standing alone can be attacked and defeated, but two can stand back-to-back and conquer. Three are even better, for a triple-braided cord is not easily broken.

(Ecclesiasteses 4:9:12) Life Recovery Bible

Before Griffin even takes a seat, I say right away, that I want to forgive my husband of all his harm. Despite his awesome sarcastic, proud, and honorary ways since the divorce, I need to caringly dismiss him out of my life. And I want to do it God's way. So first I want to make amends *with my husband*, not *to my husband*, because he is unwelcoming of me, as step nine declares: *Do not make amends, if to do so may be harmful toward another*. So I must make my conscience thoughts of amends through Griffin. Otherwise, I believe if I have harmed anyone during my abuse, especially my family, I have repeatedly asked for their forgiveness. Although it means much more to them now that they see me truly sober.

Of most priority is to make amends with myself. I am thinking back of anyone I may have hurt other than myself since my sobriety when I was in my fear, anxiety, and anger mode. I was taking my emotional withdrawals from using and my emotional withdrawals from my marriage out on other people. And these people I have called and asked for their understanding, and also told them that I would try to go forward in our conversations, leaving out the past. Most of my Christian sisters do not want to hear about my divorce, just about how well I have progressed living on my own. This is difficult, because I find myself wanting to complain. But I cannot bring others down. This is not truly representing the Steps of Recovery. So I try to think before I act and talk. And I try now more than ever to keep my commitment to others.

Since I knew that Griffin has been a sponsor to several people in the Program, I wanted to express to him special points of appreciation that I have come to truly respect about the A.A. and N.A. Programs.

On my way strolling with Griffin to his building, I once again begin to talk, always aware that I only have so much time to get in so much information.

So as we are walking toward our usual meeting area, I verbally commend various contributions of certain members of the Programs that I wanted Griffin to know about, and to the readers of this book to know about.

Jan:

"Griffin, because as you know I am journaling our talks to publish my testimony, I did not want to forget to thank certain sponsors that have helped me during my A.A. and N.A. meetings. After I fell the first time around coming out of my first rehab program, the sponsors welcomed me back with open arms. Instead of yelling at me, or reprimanding me, which I felt they had every right to do, they picked me right up, and said: 'Don't worry about it—just get right back to Step 1 and start again. Penny was one of my greatest sponsors & friends. She is the most dedicated and caring sponsor I have ever known in the Program.

"Those who chair the meetings that may have not seen me for awhile had no condemnation toward me. They just expressed an appreciation for me coming back. When the regular members of A.A. and N.A. meetings tell you: 'to keep coming back,' they sincerely mean it. This has been proven to me over and over again. I have never felt bad about walking into a meeting that I may not have attended consecutively. I had to be sure this book recognized these very special volunteers. They do not get paid for chairing the meetings—it is their way of 'giving back.' This is where I want to be at least six months to one year from now. I want to volunteer more for the cause of recovery. I have volunteered for the environment and for the homeless, and other good causes, but not yet for the 12 Steps of Recovery.

"I just pray God puts me in a place where he can use me to give back now to those who have helped make me sober and helped me to remain sober.

"The people who chair the meetings—they continue to testify how they are struggling, even after years of being sober. These are the kind of statements that really make you want to stick it out. They never pacify you that things will be easy on the road to recovery, but they do say that the recovery will become easier as long as you stay on the right track.

"I can say that things are becoming easier for me now that I am finally staying sober. When you go to meetings, sometimes aching and sweating from withdrawals, because you could not get your fix, and you had to go to a meeting because you simply did not know what to do with yourself, you can share your feelings with the members. You can let them know you have slipped back to Step 1, and it is OK with them. They understand. They really understand. It is a bit different than talking to church group members.

"That is why Griffin, in my recipe for recovery, I include a must for both To Do's: 12 Step Program through A.A. and N.A., and a church recovery program. With both of these programs, you get a variety of support and a variety of perspective that you need to booster your recovery struggles. The more active in groups you become, the less bored you will be of remaining sober. You do not want your sobriety to ever be boring. But it is totally up to how much of yourself you are willing to give.

"Griffin, I believe with those people I am able to amend with I have done so. I lost my pride, although to my character defense I was never really a proud person. I was told ever since I was a young child that I was humble. That is why I mentioned earlier that the Steps make sense to me. They make sense to me to live a happy life in general. People in general should be humble enough to admit when they're wrong and to have the humility to apologize to people they have taken their frustrations out on.

"It is only natural to me that this Step along with all the Steps will be a definite life time of re-commit on a daily basis. There is no other way. We are human, we are weak, and we are fighting our self-centered ways and selfish ways everyday. You get better, but you never get perfect.

"Actually Griffin, we can go right in to Step Nine, because I think I have already professed my following Step Eight throughout our sessions. Or am I off track here? Am I giving myself too many 'kudos'?"

Griffin:

"You do make it sound easier than what it actually is—which I can say I do admire your self-confidence. That is a sign that you are improving. But just be careful not to become over-confident. There are other ways that people can offend others than just by words. Look out for people who may be shy and need help, but just do not know how to ask. It is your duty to serve the Program if you are truly committed to the Program.

"I know you have serious physical ailments attacking you now, but I still want you to try to make more meetings. I still do not feel your meeting agenda is as full as it should be.

"I want you to try to make a list of those harms that you may have done since as far back as you can remember. And I want you to email this to me. Because there could be important events that you may not have thought of, but are hidden in your sub-conscience that could trigger you to use—and you will not even know why—but there may have been other events like when you were in the first grade that you spoke of, where you lost your self-esteem, that happened as you grew up into your adolescent years through your high school years into your womanhood years.

"For example, I believe you have made some mistakes with Herm that really hurt you today. These mistakes you have hidden by drinking. Since your relationship included fighting, there may be other strong hurts that you have to rectify within you, and possibly with Herm. I just want you to realize that Step 8 is not as easy as you make it sound. So I am giving you homework to make a thorough list of your life and the most traumatic or embarrassing events that attacked you, or how you may have attacked others, and email it to me, Ok?"

Jan:

"Actually events did come to my mind that are truly hidden deep within me. I would rather not journal them for publishing, but I will journal them for covering all my scars for my recovery to be as honest as possible. Thanks Griffin. I will do that email and send it over. But it may take a few days and nights to write."

We spend the time left talking about my abstinence from emailing or calling my ex-husband. I needed his encouragement, even though he wants me to move pass the marriage reconciliation attempts. He complemented that I remove my wedding ring by no-show of his wedding ring. He said that was a sign of my accepting my independence. And he did say, the longer you go without corresponding with the 'ex', the more you are coming to rely on God. That made sense to me. What could my 'ex' give me that God could not? There is so much more God will give you if you just put ALL your faith in Him. He helped me out of my poverty-stricken summer. He helped me to find new friends and the right doctors. Yes, God definitely is more reliable than any person could ever be. I do not want to be a hypocrite any longer. And for some time, I do feel that I was a hypocrite to my church and my other recovery groups. These probably are elements of deep remorse that I must amend too that I am now just thinking of . . . and I take it to the computer later that day—before commencing to sleep.

I think Griffin's idea of making the list is a great idea. I am already realizing important factors that I did that has harmed my self-esteem and affected my using, that I never thought of before.

So sometimes even the 12 Steps of Recovery appears simple, it really is not. The more honest you are with the Program, the more difficult it will be—because you will want to do more work for your recovery—no matter how much it hurts to take the band-aids off the scars.

Step Nine

WE MADE DIRECT AMENDS TO SUCH PEOPLE WHEREVER POSSIBLE, EXCEPT WHEN TO DO SO WOULD INJURE THEM OR OTHERS.

So if you are presenting a sacrifice at the altar in the Temple and you suddenly remember that someone has something against you, leave your sacrifice there at the altar. Go and be reconciled to that person. Then come and offer your sacrifice to God. When you are on your way to court with your adversary, settle your differences quickly. Otherwise, your accuser may hand you over to the judge, who will hand you over to an officer, and you will be thrown into prison.

(Matthew 5 23-25) Life Recovery Bible

Jan:

"My husband has a difficult time with accepting my way of amending to him. I have amended to him over and over again. But what he returns to me is judgmental behavior against me, and constant inventory of MY wrongs. And as mentioned earlier, I will not mention his addictive behaviors in this book; because it is about Jan and Jan's recovery. But Griffin, my ex-husband had major addictions, that he never apologized for, let alone go to rehab for; and that is my ongoing anger issue with him. But despite that, I told him I was willing to come back and work out his faults with a counselor or a marriage counseling pastor. And he refused. That was and will be my last email of correspondence to him.

"He was not there when I needed just a friend. So I got over it. I forgave him for the abandonment. But God will judge one day, and that is what gives me the peace of mind and spirit that I need to fulfill my future. He may not admit it, but he knows exactly what I am talking about, if he were to read this book.

"It seems that trying to amend with him hurts him. So do I abide by Step Nine, and stop amending with him for now, since it is hurtful to him? In my heart though, I know it is hurtful to him, because he knows the wrong he did. Although I admit my wrong, whenever I bring up 'his wrongs' he is short-tempered and tells me: 'tell it to the shrink.'

"So how do you deal with that?

"I was able to amend with all the others I feel I hurt in my alcoholism or drug addictions. But with him, it is hard to even have a conversation even if a pastor is mediating between us. So this step in one that is most difficult to succeed beyond without one of the most important people in your life. So I just amend to whom and where I can, and then look to proceed to Step Ten.

"I recently made a call and said I was sorry for scolding him on deceiving me with how he arranged the divorce. He divorced me on my birthday, and said he would probably re-marry me on my next birthday, and that did not happen.

"A pastor that we seen after the divorce advised him to take me out once a week to try to reconcile our marriage, and he did not follow through, but continued to ignore and abandon me.

"Although this transpired on his initiative or his non-initiative, I decided to call to say I was sorry for hurting him with destructive words. I felt this was necessary for me to be true to my Steps of Recovery.

"He now just wants to live single and carefree. I must accept this, although according to doctors, he is the cause of my recent health decline, both mentally and physically.

"Nonetheless, if I am to be honest with the Steps of Recovery, I must let it go, and let what he has done go. Although I apologized to him many times for hurting him while I was married to him, I felt a need to verbalize a sincere sorry to him again in respect to my going beyond Step Nine of the Program.

"But to be honest with myself and the Program, I believe I will be climbing Step Nine for the rest of my life with him. I do not believe I am the only person that may take a lifetime to make amends with someone who you feel hurt you so badly that forgiveness will take perhaps a lifetime to achieve. I do not want to leave this Earth without forgiving him, so I pray it happens sooner than later. But, again, to be honest with the Program, he is the only person that I as of yet cannot sincerely make amends with, and not because of his divorcing me, but because of how he handled the divorce. He abandoned me 100 percent. Upon asking for $10 when I was broke, he did not mind me turning to the alternative, and that was to go to a blood bank to sell my blood. But even this 'let down' did not pull me down into the abyss of using. And thank you God for that with my whole heart and soul.

"A man should never divorce his wife on her birthday, and then encourage her to make it all up by remarrying her on her birthday the following year—and then not follow through. I did not go to court to fight the divorce because I believed him when he said that God is bigger than any piece of court paper. He also told me that he would stick around and not abandon me. But what he assured me that he would do to ease my pain upon leaving our home, is not what resulted. He divorced me on May 20, 2009 and said he would probably remarry me on May 20, 2010, but as I write this book in the winter weather of 2010, I now have to accept what has not happened, and go on with my life.

"So although as loyal A.A. and N.A. members, we must re-commit to the Steps of Recovery daily, I will give extra effort to making it through Step Nine by sincerely forgiving him. I emailed and phoned him my forgiveness, but then the next day, I would negate what I said, and continue to put shame, blame, and guilt upon him. This was getting me no where in my recovery or in my marriage reconciliation. He does accept some of the blame, but not at the level that I believe he should. So that is why, I must be honest in my testimony of my recovery by acknowledging that I have not yet successfully made it through Step Nine.

"So as I write this book this day, December 14, 2010, it has been two months since I sent him an email of a marriage counseling pastor to call for our possible reconciliation. I am sober. I have not been angry with him. I have not sent any shaming or blaming emails. So why does he refuse to call the pastor I recommended. Why? I know why. He wants to live single. So what can I do or say? I must accept his choice of life and how he wants to live it. And just go on. But what I should not do is wait on him. But when you follow Scripture as carefully as I do, it does say in Ephesians and Corinthians, that I am his wife and he is my husband by God, unless one of us remarries (thus, committing adultery) or one of us expires, that is, dies. So if I meet someone that cares for me, it may be difficult for me to ever remarry by God's New Testament instructions. As far as him, I am clueless.

"But as it says in the *Little Red Book,* that A.A. and N.A. members are familiar with, Step Nine may be a Step that truly is never fully climbed or overcome."

Griffin:

"I understand your position in how you stand on the Step Nine demands. It is not easy for someone in your position; and I like how you are still trying to reconcile for peace of mind for yourself. And I am proud that you still go forward with the remaining Steps of Recovery. Just because you cannot get pass Step Nine does not mean that you should stop and give up on the Program. And as I put on the hat of your AA sponsor, I congratulate you for re-committing to them everyday.

"Also, you may not think of it now, but perhaps there are hidden anger issues with other loved ones or acquaintances, besides your 'ex', that you must also resolve issues with. There may be underlying damages from others in your past relationships that are also holding you back from achieving Step Nine.

"And be prepared that you may be on Step Nine regarding amending with the 'ex' for the rest of your life. But if you can forgive him, and he likewise forgives you, perhaps you may not reconcile for marriage, but you could allow each other to continue your lives without holding resentment against each other.

"Is he aware of the Steps of Recovery, since you would not mention which addictive behaviors he had, but you did say that he did suffer with addictive behaviors—so has he been through the Steps of Recovery Program?"

Jan:

"In this book, I am limiting sharing his involvement to the Recovery Program by only stating that he is loyal to Alanon, which does teach the recovery walk using similar Bible supplements."

Griffin:

"O.K. good, then perhaps you and he can leave each other in your own independent walk of life without anger or resentment. These must be relief from your systems. Perhaps the longer the separation, the healthier time you both will have to forgive and to go on—to go forward for your work for God. You said that he was a Christian man. And I know you are a Christian woman. So you both hopefully will be healed over time. Who knows what God's plans may be for both of you, but you must get through Step Nine between each. You both have extended your respect to Step Nine in light of each other's hurt and pain, so that is good. But you do not want the anger to rekindle, so that is why we must recommit to the Steps all the time. Emotions can bring us down when tragedies happen, and we may look to blame someone, but this is not living the Steps. The days of your blaming anyone, including the ex-husband, are over! How do you feel about that?"

Jan:

"I will not allow him or others, whether new friends or old friends from holding me back from climbing to the top of Step Nine. Sometimes I wished there were more friends that had called me or reached out to me, but I still cannot be upset. Others have issues and problems in their own lives that I must be aware of . . . and expecting them to feel sorry for me . . . is only dwelling in my self-pity, selfishness, and self-centeredness.

"God has given me two dependable Christian friends to share my sufferings by upholding discussions in a sharing kind of way. I do not focus only on myself, but I will ask my sister about how I can help in her life. She is one of the two special friends that God has held by my side throughout my trauma of drug and alcohol abuse.

"And my new friend, Sharon, I do not want to lean on too much either. I try to get out of myself by asking her if I can run errands for her elderly mother's strict diet. One day I went to pick up some sort of unique oatmeal that her mother is restricted under doctor's orders to eat. I felt good that I was able to help another, during the turmoil of my pain.

"One of the greatest gifts, Griffin, of the Steps, is how the Program encourages you to get out of yourself, and give to others, and to other good causes; this is where I am now. I want to give this book to the rehab centers as an encouragement for other users to come out and seek walking a Christian life; and then I want and pray that God places me where my skills can best be used for His purposes."

Griffin and I went for coffee to talk a bit more since we finished about a half hour earlier with the session. He allowed me to treat him to a bagel and coffee. I felt so good that I talked about everything BUT my husband. And as good as he is—he recognized that I did not include my pity talk and said that I am becoming more independent. I felt good walking home that day. I actually did not even catch the train—I walked all the way that evening from downtown.

There were lights going up all over downtown; we were now in Christmas pre-season. I enjoyed all the beautiful lights and watching those workers who delicately put them in place. It comforted me to view the complacency in these people who smiled as they watched the lights spectacularly illuminate the already beautifully architecturally structured buildings of the Chicago downtown skyline. I was grateful to God. I looked forward to seeing my cat, Samson, as I do when I first walk in my apartment. I was glad to have a roof over my head, a warm bed to sleep in, and an animal waiting for me who depended on me. Life was becoming better by the day.

It is o.k. that my husband is not here to celebrate my recovery. What I now feel in my heart, is that he may not have meant to stay away so long, but people change. Depending what is going on in their lives—people can change. So perhaps I should not condemn him for being deceitful or misleading. I do not know what caused the unexpected change in his behavior. Each person has an individual identity & chemistry that uniquely re-acts to the circumstances of life and uncomprehensible by anyone other than God. Step Nine allows me to amend with him through God—and Step Nine enables me to trust that God will intervene to either re-unite us or retain our separation for His Purpose in our lives. So I want to climb to the top of Step Nine *amending to those I hurt through God—asking God to make it turn out to His desires and not our individual desires. Thank you God.*

Later that evening I called Griffin, as he has allowed me to do in the past. I wanted to talk more about the nervous breakdowns I had suffered since moving three times in one year since the divorce. Eventually the most recent of the breakdowns placed me in the emergency room of the closet hospital.

I truly believe my first nervous breakdown was the Valentines Day following my sobriety month. I tried to perform a classroom teaching lesson to attain a fellowship into the public school teaching arena, but I could barely write my name on the chalkboard before giving my history lesson to fellow peers sitting in the classroom in front of me. And as mentioned prior, I overlooked parts of the exam. These events followed my sobriety, and thanks to God did not take away my sobriety. I am grateful they did not take me back to the dark side.

Being alone and in poverty, left me no choice but to walk for every need, even to the downtown CEDA office to get hardship funding to keep my electric going. These are traumatic experiences that still hurt so deeply, and evade my overcoming Step Nine, especially concerning my ex-husband.

I am wrong to blame him or any other person for the aftermath of the divorce. Was it his fault that I lived an entire summer in poverty? Is it anyone's fault that I have arthritis now in my legs from so much extensive moving in a short time? I want to place the blame to some extent on him, but perhaps that is not God's desire. I must remember the monies I spent to support my habit, and return this bad behavior outcome against me and not against him.

I have to examine my forgiveness to him and to others each time I want to place blame somewhere. I understand my ex-husband needed peace and had to stay away to have that peace. He may have led me to believe that he would be around more, but his mental and emotional needs changed. I must see this in order to forgive him. I am grateful for his help with one year rent and with COBRA health insurance. I must focus on the good that he did, and not on what he found himself unable to do for me.

As I sat in the yard day after day over the past summer in my most recent apartment where I now reside, I can attest to knowing, to truly knowing, what it feels like to be alone. This makes me want to reach out to others who suffer from being alone. I owned no car to get around. So I walked everywhere for me, as well as for the needs of my aunt. I was grateful to my parents for taking me on errands more than I deserved, and for offering to take my cat to the veterinarian. I guess I feel angry at my ex-husband for placing burdens on my elderly parents. But again, is this his fault that I was non-efficient or non-independent during the marriage and after the marriage?

When I felt anger about my situation, I recall glancing at unusual happenings in the yard, such as seeing these hard-shelled rock-looking bugs on top of locusts. These two bugs would be surrounding the side door of the yard as I walked out each morning with my cat, Samson. I had never seen two entirely different bug species so close as if they were mating. I was thinking could this be a sign of bad things to come for me? This represented chaos, but I wanted peace. As I watched this in distress almost every morning in the later part of July through the mid part of August, I prayed for God to bring me peaceful signs.

Then I recall how butterflies began to somehow land on leaves that would be hanging close to me, and each time the butterfly remained on the leaf until I pet it. I felt that God was now giving me a sign of His peace.

I knew God was with me. God gave me signs that He will oppress the oppressors.

I needed to let Griffin know the hardest times come back to me still now, the horrific memories. And yet I must get over Step Nine and stop the blame of anyone. I should have prepared more for the divorce. I must extend my ex-husband forgiveness, because I know it is the godly perspective. God wants me to have peace, not chaos. Step Nine delivers peace, such as the sign of the butterfly allowing me to stroke its beautiful wings. Without Step Nine, I may see ugly creatures that have hard rock formations, and that represents chaos.

I needed to share with Griffin these signs that appeared as I struggled with forgiveness. Yes, I want the butterflies more and more. I want the beauty of God's peace. I want to remain past Step Nine.

Step Ten

WE CONTINUED TO TAKE PERSONAL INVENTORY AND WHEN WE WERE WRONG PROMPTLY ADMITTED IT.

Purify me from my sins, and I will be clean; wash me, and I will be whiter than snow. Oh, give me back my joy again; you have broken me—now let me rejoice. Don't keep looking at my sins. Remove the stain of my guilt. Create in me a clean heart O God; renew a loyal spirit within me.

(Psalm 51:7-10) Life Recovery Bible

Griffin and I have decided for our Step Ten meeting to do something a bit different in terms of our meeting place. Instead of meeting at our usual office setting, he decided that we would go "dutch" and meet in a nice restaurant over lunch. It was actually one of my favorite restaurants, and I did not recall ever mentioning to him how much I favored this restaurant. I can't help but think somehow this man is clairvoyant—could I ask for a better therapist. He even picks out my favorite place to eat—that's pretty cool—I think. So I meet him sitting near a sun shining place of the restaurant which adds more optimism to the environment. He seems to always get it right—and as I take my seat to a smiling invitation—I relax and begin to talk—because no matter where the place—I am still on the clock.

Jan:

"Well I have admitted my faults to my A.A. and N.A. members, as well as my grievance group, and now I feel sort of naked in the sense that I have exposed all that I need help in dealing with my sobriety stability.

"I am still angry with myself, and I know that I was at fault for most of the demise of the marriage through my outbursts upon my husband.

"Now I catch myself when I am doing the same in outbursts toward my mother or father. It's as if the worse shortcomings during sobriety newness are fear and anger.

"If I have left other faults out, at this time, I am not aware of it. But I know if I acknowledge other unintentional hidden faults, I will be more than willing to relieve those oppressions by admitting my need of help. It is a good feeling to share, but to share only with those who want you to share.

"It does hurt quite severely that at one time my husband was very interested in each 'baby step' of my recovery. But now, he says: 'Tell it to the therapist or the counselor or the pastor.' So I still must get stronger in my control to not feel a need to tell him what is going on with my progress. I do not want to go so far as to say that he does not care. I do not know what goes on in his head."

Griffin:

"Jan, as hard as it is for me to tell you again, but yes, forget the ex! He is out of your life . . . for now. You cannot expect him to come back. Because if you are waiting for him, you are putting your full recovery on hold too; and that is dangerous. You must think of your life now as a single woman who can make it in life with a solid working network of sober good people who support and love you.

"And that is what you have been doing. Now, if you are telling me that you must stop communicating with him, then I can only expect that you might have been talking or emailing him while seeing me. And if you have, I am not going to scold you. But it must completely stop. He seems to me that he no longer cares about you at all. Now, I may also not know what goes on in his head, but actions speak for someone's true feelings. And I think your husband has given up all together on you. But if you are to go forward with living the 12 Steps of Recovery, you must put behind you the shame, the blame, and the guilt. Like we discussed, you may never truly amend with him, but you tried, and that is all that counts in points toward your integrity in following through with the Program."

Jan:

"Griffin, thank you for telling me like it is. I do not expect any false comforting from you. And you have only been honest with me since our start of seeing each other in our therapy sessions. I do appreciate that very much. Now let us forget him, and talk about my shortcomings that I do notice and try to rectify immediately in my recovery walk.

"I do notice I still have anger and self-pity matters, but not to the degree that I first had when I became sober almost one year ago. Another shortcoming that I try to resolve when I catch it occurring in my way of interactions with others, is cancelling on commitments that I make for meetings, or for certain events. I am trying hard now to stick to what I commit to, so that others will see me as dependable.

"I recall in various A.A. and N.A. meetings, people testifying to the embarrassment of being told by their friends or loved ones that they could not be depended on—well, that was me too! My parents once said: 'Jan, you always cancel at the last minute, so we just now take it as it comes.' And I must admit Griffin that made me feel bad, and shallow. So what I am trying to acknowledge in our session today, is that I hope to truly see myself for how I am, without covering up things that need to be corrected."

Griffin:

"Jan, the more sober you remain, the more you will come to terms with your character flaws, but you will be willing and wanting to resolve them. You have a new revelation for the feelings of others and their way of perceiving you. You are out of the self-centered and selfish realm. Although fear may come and go, you have your faith to overcome. You are stronger in your faith that truly helps you carry on progressively through the Program. What you have coming in to sobriety that other patients of mine do not have, is this life long faith in God, and the conviction that has stayed within you since you were a small child. God will not let you go. And you will not let God go."

Jan:

"Sometimes I find it hard to move from various A.A. and N.A. meetings due to my apartment moves, but due to the common morale of the leaders at these various clubs, it is not so bad. There is a renewed anxiety that I will be accepted. Certain meetings now are sort of far for me to get to without a car, so

I have to go to closer places. So it is hard to make friendships that have to fade when you cannot see certain people. But I am still trying to maintain a building network through such technological sophistications as email, etc. So I should be OK with moving around."

Griffin:

"Hey, look at it as optimistic and another blessing from God. More people get to hear your exciting testimony one day. I know you said you have not given a 'talk' since the rehab stays. But keep going, and one day, various A.A. and N.A. leaders will invite you to speak at their clubs. And that could not be a better way to come back and say hi to friends."

Jan:

"Thanks Griffin, and by the way, the food is great. Come on let me pay the tab, and you get the tip. Consider it a holiday gift. Would that be O.K.?"

Griffin:

"O.K. Jan, I accept."

Walking home from the restaurant, I feel that I do not need to tell him everything that is going on with me in all my variations of health matters; I know that will help me. But, Griffin, being a man, makes it hard to explain some of the woman health regressions that do affect my sobriety strength. I'd rather not discuss these personal issues in this book, but let us just say I am in physical therapy now at Loyola Hospital. I hope it goes well. I perhaps inherited some woman area physical ailments that my mother suffered with; but since she came out O.K., I am hoping the same progress for myself. I worry a bit as I walk, because I know tomorrow will be painful in the therapy that I am undergoing at Loyola. But I want more than anything to first be a good Christian for God's work, and secondly, to be a full woman. It is important to me to feel like a full woman.

This therapy at Loyal is supposed to correct some problems I had that I feel did intrude upon my marriage as well as other matters that were revealed during my sessions with Griffin. But, I think it is not necessary to tell Griffin some of these matters. It even may make him feel a bit uncomfortable. Then a thought comes to my mind that I did have a pastor's wife give me her phone number to call her for personal advice; so that night I go home and that is exactly what I do. I use the network of strong stable people that God has blessed me with—I am learning how to reach out more and more. You know, I think the greatest part of the 12 Steps of Recovery has taught me how to not be afraid to reach out for help as much as necessary. God gives us the tools—but we need to use the tools before they get rusty.

Now I rush a bit faster to go home. I am looking forward to speaking with my new friend, Susan, Baptist pastor Steve Rust's wife. And if she is unavailable, I will call my friend Sharon from across the street. I like how I am getting away from the comfortableness of feeling isolated. I am slowly understanding why A.A. and N.A. enforce people to get out, to get with others, and to not be isolated. I am taking it a step further. Besides getting away from being isolated in my activities, I am getting away from being isolated in my thoughts. This is good progress, and brings a smile of contentment to my face that now has sparkles of snow caressing it. I take a skip, and thank God for the beginning of a new life. So I have to go forward and strengthen myself to communicate with those in my group, and my therapist. Right now, they are the proper "sounding board" for my progressions and regressions.

Step Eleven

WE SOUGHT THROUGH PRAYER AND MEDITATION TO IMPROVE OUR CONSCIOUS CONTACTS WITH GOD, PRAYING ONLY FOR KNOWLEDGE OF HIS WILL FOR US AND THE POWER TO CARRY THAT OUT.

"There is no judgment against anyone who believes in Him. But anyone who does not believe in Him has already been judged for not believing in God's one and only Son. And the judgment is based on this fact: God's light came into the world, but people loved the darkness more than the light, for their actions were evil. All who do evil hate the light and refuse to go near it for fear their sins will be exposed. But those who do what is right come to the light so others can see that they are doing what God wants."

(John 3:18:21) Life Recovery Bible

Griffin:

"Jan, I think you thought after Illinois rehab you were doing your treatment finally for you. But I think you were doing it more to reconcile your marriage. What is important now is that you are seeing how you may have deceived yourself. You are making great progress. The most important reception you can return to the Steps of A.A. and N.A. is honesty and humility. And you are doing that, and continually admitting where you may have been deceived by your own love for your husband. You want to stop any more co-dependency on him now!

"I am proud of you. So let's see. You are challenging your low self-esteem, your people-pleasing and now ALL your co-dependencies. You have talked of your family, but now we are seeing the ex-husband as a new co-dependency, and it is coming from your own observation, and that is really genuine progress.

"I want you to repeatedly read through the *The Little Red Book* that supplements the Steps of A.A., We may be able to finally forgive the ex-husband, and that may be the true breakthrough to going forward with relieving a huge core reason that could interfere with your substance dependencies now! Right now, you have a lot of anger against what he did to you. It is normal for you to have this anger, but it still must be diminished for you to truly go forward with Jan's progress in the Recovery Steps of A.A."

Jan:

"Ok Griffin. I'll review the readings. But just so you know I have recently volunteered to shovel for the landlord, who is handicapped, to give of myself. It also energizes my health.

"I do feel great when I am doing good deeds for others. It prevents me from lonely feelings and motivates me that I can still do useful favors to help others . . . to help me get out of myself.

"I agree by my own experience, the more you give of yourself to others, the better you feel spiritually, emotionally, and physically.

"I'm leaving early now to go shovel his two properties. So I'll catch you later over the phone for my next hour."

Griffin:

"Good, I like that! Go carry out your commitment. I hope you have a warm pair of gloves."

As I walk away, I show him my work gloves, and he returns a content smile.

Step Twelve

HAVING HAD A SPIRITUAL AWAKENING AS A RESULT OF THESE STEPS, WE TRIED TO CARRY THIS MESSAGE TO OTHERS AND TO PRACTICE THESE PRINCIPLES IN ALL OUR AFFAIRS.

You won't spend the rest of your lives chasing your own desires, but you will be anxious to do the will of God. You have had enough in the past of the evil things that godless people enjoy—their immorality and lust, their feasting and drunkenness and wild parties, and their terrible worship of idols. Of course, your former friends are surprised when you no longer plunge into the flood of wild and destructive things they do. So they slander you. But remember that they will have to face God, who will judge every one, both the living and the dead. That is why the Good News was preached to those who are now dead—so although they were destined to die like all people, they now live forever with God in the Spirit.

(1Peter 4:2-6) Life Recovery Bible

Since today we are going through the last Step, I decide that I want to share my miracles from God with Griffin. This is something I do not do with many people, but because he believes in my faith in God, I want to share these most beautiful events with him—to give him a gift back—for the gift of these sessions that he has given me. I do believe Griffin may have also received miracles from God.

So upon walking to his office, where he already is taking his ritual notes—I just burst out and say:

Jan:

"Griffin, it is time for you to be a witness by my words of the miracles that God has done in my life. I want you to receive my sharing of these miracles as a gift from me to you that your faith will grow in God. You have helped me to regain more faith so I want to do the same for you.

"I want to go from most present miracles to the earliest miracles from God upon my life. First, by God's intervention, I have recovered from two major addictions simultaneously. Even though the aches and the sweats were still with me for a long time to come on and off, because you cannot depend on Suboxone to relieve all the withdrawal symptoms. And I definitely could not turn to Suboxone to take away the hurt, I turned to God to relieve the pains of withdrawal of the marriage. God released me from the chains of bondage that was tearing me to shreds. God worked two miracles in my life—He took me off from the addictions without going to an insane asylum or to my grave and He made me a strong woman to handle the pain of being abandoned. He now works in me to help others to overcome and to know that God has a purpose for us, and not to feel defeated or worthless. The divorce does not make me a failure, but a survivor!

"The miracle prior to this was the safekeeping of my cat, Samson, during the worse storms of my life. Living alone, and realizing as I was still withdrawing from my addictions from the aftermath of new realizations that come upon you—the character flaws you now have to deal with on life's terms—I and Samson were alone for most of the 24 hours of each soaring hot day—and God was with us. He carried us through poverty. We had no money, and hardly no way of getting around. I had two real physical ailments that hit me hard from moving so harshly too often. Sometimes I did not know what to do but cry out to God to be with me and to take my place in life. He did just that. He sent me His Helper, the Holy Spirit and a special guardian angel to watch over my roaming cat who I love dearly. One cat unfortunately did die on the street, and I picked up his little head and placed him in a box. I wept knowing how easily it could have been my cat, my Samson.

"During my first rehab in Florida when it was utterly impossible for me to go to sleep, I prayed for God to blanket me with His Holy Spirit so that I could sleep and awake for the sake of my health. I knew without rest I would not make the 28 day Program. That same night after sincerely, faithfully praying that God was listening, I just knocked out like that at 10:20 or 10:30 pm, and awoke at 5:50 am the next morning. This miracle would occur each night until I graduated the Program.

"Not long ago before I married, my father's cat was gone for 10 days without food or water. We found out later he was locked up in a garage. I asked my family to gather around the table where we were eating breakfast, and to put their hands within each other's hands and pray in agreement to God through Jesus that He bring my dad's beloved cat home. Later that afternoon, my father called to tell me his cat, Tabby, walked through the kitchen door unharmed.

"God saved me from PCP as I testified to you earlier, a drug that put me in the most vulnerable positions that could have killed me. He rescued me and gave me guardian angels. I do believe there are many different angels for different purposes. God uses angels to complete his miracles, and He did so with me. When an intoxicated man tried to hurt me by inviting me to babysit at his apartment, where I would later find out there was no baby to be babysat, God sent an angel to fight this man off of me. I prayed for God to save me in front of this demonic drunken person who was much taller than myself, and not a second later God sent me an angel with strength to push the man down away from me, and later this man was placed in a mental institution.

"This was shortly after God rescued me from PCP, and I knew He would save me again. This time I prayed in the name of Christ, because I was just saved at a Bible Study at the age of 17, and we learn when we accept Christ as our Personal Savior, that we always come to the Lord in the name of Christ. That is what I did, and God made sure not one part of my body was harmed.

"This miracle is actually when I was in my early 20s. So I am a bit out of chronological order. Forgive me. But when my Aunt Sue, who was a special beautiful soul, was stricken with heart failure to the painful pressure of her organs failing and her body bloating to an unrecognizable shape, and the doctor said she would need surgery to stop the inside bleeding; I talked to her that night of Heaven and of us all going there someday. She was mildly retarded but she understood. I asked her if she wanted the pain to stop and to continue our lives in Heaven. I promised her that she would be with me someday in Heaven. She said, 'Janice I do not want any knives. Yes, I want the angels.' My father called me at 1:30 AM the next morning to tell me that God had taken Aunt Sue during her sleep.

"As I testified earlier to you, there was the miracle of saving me from my first day of torment at school when the teacher cut my hair. How was I ever to go back, but I prayed as a six-year old for God to restore me to at least face the students the next day, and He did."

Griffin:

"Without much thought, I have a feeling that your friend, Sharon, may be your latest miracle. And the groups that you are now rising above your self-pity to reach out and give others your strengths and talents to see them happy. This I feel is your latest miracle from God.

"Through your groups, your friends, and me, God is helping you to reach out to others to get out of your own sorrows and depression. I would recommend whatever God places on your heart to do in service to others, whether it be the homeless, the sick, the nursing home visits, or even with animal type of rescue help, do it! The more you get of yourself and express this to others in testimony to your recovery peers, the more you will be showing them how our Lord works in others to do His Will. You must continue to exemplify how much God has helped you—your recovery is too great to keep to yourself. And I think the book testimony is a good start of sharing what the 12 Steps of Recovery have done in your life through God."

Jan:

"Griffin, you know me as well as I know myself. And right now, you just verified that. And what perfect timing to verify that, at our Step 12. Yes, Sharon, is actually teaching me how to reach out to help others whether it is a ministry through the Central Assembly of God, or whether it is individual ministry work I have been led to do through prayer and meditation to my Father God.

"Also a new friend God had blessed me with to get me through the most devastating time of my life I must not forget. She is my landlady and very good friend, Milica Trutin, who encouraged me that I was a beautiful person with a beautiful personality. If it was not for her seeing me alone everyday in the backyard, I bet I would have never been able to finish this book. So yes, God brought the few special right people just at the most needy time of my life. And to Milica, I am most grateful and must express this. I am learning a lot from observing her hard work in her beautiful garden. To see how she joyfully observes how her vegetables grow, and how she observes them in sincere appreciation—I have never witnessed before. These small beauties of life, you notice when you are sober. This is a true joy. And I am glad that I am well enough to enjoy my sobriety to notice these small things from people that are actually huge thanksgivings to God. Milica, like my parents, never did drugs or smoked cigarettes, and yet the joy she has in watching her vegetables grow, to me, is the true beauty of life. You won't get it though, unless you are sober!

"How did you know that Sharon was leading me into reaching out to others for God?"

Griffin:

"Well, for example, you earlier said that she encouraged you to help initiate the grief meeting for women. Although your depression was still a bit too deep, it was a joy for you to suggest the idea at the church meeting, and then for the pastor to bless you with Nona as your leader. This is reaching out and giving back. This is what Step 12 is about, and you are doing it—you are doing it!"

Griffin and I have been six weeks in session, going through each step at each meeting, with reassurance that we will continue to go through the Steps again and again, until he feels confident in me that I am living the Steps each day of my life.

I feel good that Griffin cares enough about me to care that I take the A.A. and N.A. Steps of Recovery very seriously. He did email me that he wants me to suggest offering to give my testimony or speaker talk at those meetings that will allow me to do so. I am so afraid to do that yet, but the journaling of this book is a sure start.

Although he is a male therapist, I was comfortable in sharing with him other ailments that are not withdrawal, but feel like withdrawal because of the hot and cold flashes that come upon a woman when she is experiencing the "change of life." But it is hard to tell because according to my own research as a woman, these are change of life side effects and must not be confused with withdrawal symptoms.

I also have other physical woman issues to deal with, that may require surgery, but I am glad if it makes me "whole" again. Women go through more changes as they grow older than men in various physical elements of their physical chemistry.

I am now seeing a woman therapist soley regarding my more personal womanhood ailments, and I hope one day to be cured. The therapist tells me that the exercises may be able to pre-empt the need for surgery. I hope so.

The sobriety in my life now enables me to go through my physical or emotional or mental struggles alone and with courage.

Once you are over your fear of your core flaws and have forgiven yourself—you start to love yourself—the "real you."

FINALE

My next goal after reaching out with this book is to hopefully help others with their substance or alcohol abuse recovery. For example, I hope to take my book to students after I take it to rehab centers and other places where addicts and alcoholics are seeking recovery comfort.

I want to exemplify the ugliness of drugs and alcohol to the best of my skills in caring for others. Once I know that God has given me the tools I need to carry on "speaker events" where I can share my testimony live with youngsters, and in A.A. and N.A. meetings, I will be ready to speak. This is my next goal and prayer—that I am invited to speak about the evil ways that Satan uses to tempt our youth into "partying." Not remembering your social events because you were too drunk or too drugged is NOT cool. It is the lowest disrespect for one self to indulge in a life style of drugs and drinking. To damage your body that God gave you is hurtful to your family and to God. Just think of the smart brain cells you are destroying that God meant for you to use as a chemist or as a professor. When you think more seriously before you take that first drink or drug, you just may put it back or stomp it out. I did not have the logical sense in my head that I now have. I am so grateful to see more and more educational commercials against drug and alcohol use—the commercials that make teenagers want to be happy teenagers that remember their youth.

God wants you to love yourself and your body—and that means, staying away from drinking, smoking and drugging. So now I wait for my time to witness and carry the message on to others—once I begin to do this type of service, then I will feel as a whole person for the first time in my life.

Thank you readers for sharing my testimony.